FITZGO
The Wild Dog of Central Park

❧❧❧❧❧❧❧❧❧❧

FITZGO

The Wild Dog of Central Park

❀❀❀❀❀❀❀❀❀❀❀❀❀❀❀❀❀❀❀

by PAUL WILKES

J. B. LIPPINCOTT COMPANY
Philadelphia and New York

U.S. Library of Congress Cataloging in Publication Data

Wilkes, Paul, birth date
   Fitzgo: the wild dog of Central Park.

   SUMMARY: The adventures of a stray dog that survives
by scavenging in Central Park and eventually goes to live
with the author and his wife in a brownstone in Brooklyn.
   1. Dogs—Legends and stories.   [1. Dogs]
I. Title.
SF426.2.W54   818'.5'408   73–1826
ISBN–0–397–00979–8

*For all those
who have reached out to refugees—
whether it was Fitzgo, Phil or Dan—
don't hesitate to do it again.
You know the great joy
they gave you in return.*

FITZGO
The Wild Dog of Central Park

Chapter One

NEW YORK CITY's Central Park is known for many things. In the warmer months it is a green haven in the middle of high-rise apartments, honking cabs and crowded streets. To children, its swings, its fountains of water, its rocks are welcome relief from being cooped up in the few rooms of an apartment. For adults, it is a place to relax in, a place for wandering and watching the seasons change—pleasures the paved-over, built-up city has deprived them of. But, because it is in the middle of America's largest city, Central Park is also the stalking ground for muggers and robbers, a place where someone admiring a field of daffodils may suddenly find himself sprawled in the middle of them, minus his wallet.

What so many people say about New York City might also be said about the park: "It's a nice place to visit, but I wouldn't want to live there." But live there he did.

9 &

My wife, Joy, and I don't know when the wild dog came to the park or where he came from, but once he settled into the section near where we lived, he could easily be watched from our windows on the fourth floor, which faced the park. I should quickly say that my wife was more fascinated by the dog than I. To me he was just a brown-and-white dog of average size who for some reason gave the impression of having some wolf blood. To Joy he was a gallant prince of the park, standing up to its challenges twenty-four hours a day, good weather and bad.

Unlike the wild dogs that ran in packs and were eventually conquered by the park, by cars or by the dog catcher, this dog was a loner. He had a gentle way about him, Joy tried to convince me. She saw that he never growled or snapped at people. Nor did he ever allow them close to him. Somehow he must have sensed that viciousness would end in capture and death and that if he was overfriendly he would be victimized. If he had been stupid he wouldn't have lasted a week. Central Park presents hazards in abundance. To stay alive there a dog has to learn unique ways to get food; he has to be perpetually on guard. And this dog was. His brown eyes constantly scanned the slopes. His tail was more often between his legs than up in the air, showing he knew how precarious his existence was.

"Look at him; there he is!" I'd often hear this call from Joy, and I'd drag myself away from a book or from work around the apartment to watch her dog. For recreation he chased the green Metropolitan Transport buses as they made their way along the street by the park. Yellow cabs were another challenge. But most of the cab drivers saw little charm in this wild dog, with tongue hanging out, yapping at their wheels. Some of them would stop quickly when he started to chase them, trying to get him in front of the cab to run him over. We saw many close calls from our fourth-floor window, and Joy cheered every time he escaped injury or death.

Most of the time he spent lying on top of a particular knoll, licking himself, trying to preserve some degree of cleanliness in the sooty and often muddy park. Or he would lie under a favorite bush near the edge of the park, where he could quickly retreat into the wilds or go out and play his games with buses and taxis on the street.

"He's like one of those lions in Africa," Joy said. "Confident as can be but never forgetful that danger could lurk behind the next bush. What a dog! What a perfect pet he'd make if someone could tame him."

"Uuummm," was my less than enthusiastic answer. "Just what I always wanted: a wolf," I said softly.

We first saw him when winter was coming to Central Park. When the temperature was in the 30's or 40's, he would spend most of his time in open areas where he could easily keep watch. When the icy rains and then the snows came, he spent more time in his bush, where nature or he had burrowed out a spot. The bush formed a little grotto that kept the wind and rain out but allowed him a quick exit. We had watched people try to approach him in the park and saw how quickly he escaped.

The first major snowfall came early that year, dumping four inches overnight. A snowstorm paralyzes New York City, simply because there is no place to push the snow. When Joy saw the park and streets covered the next morning, she was sure that among the normal casualties—bent fenders from accidents, people injured from shoveling—a small brown-and-white dog might have been beaten by a storm, as many before him had.

Joy moped over coffee that morning; she didn't have to work because the snow had closed all the city's schools for the day. She took the smallest sips from the cup and kept looking out the window. All she saw were yellow city snowplows slowly making their way through the streets, burying parked cars, and people trudging toward the subway through snow in drifts higher than their knees.

"He's probably okay," I said, a bit impatiently. "He's made it this far. He'll be okay."

"But this is his first big snow, his first winter in the park." Joy stood up to look out the window once more. "Who could last in that?"

"Let's be realistic. He's living on borrowed time already. Maybe it's best that . . . that something happens now. Kinder, it could be really kinder to him. Winter is brutal out there."

She sat back down and took another sip. "Somebody should take him in. Maybe we could . . ."

I put a hand on hers. "The way we travel and the way our lease reads? C'mon, be realistic."

"I am realistic. He's just like the dogs my folks had on the farm. Mutts are the best kind, they really are."

"I never had anything but hand-me-down mongrels, either. But not now, Joy, we can't be tied to a dog."

"But he's so special, Paul, so regal out there."

"And that's where he has to be. You can't domesticate something out of the wild just like that. And besides." I hesitated. "I don't like the looks of him. He scares me."

The cold held the snow intact throughout the day, but by evening the street alongside the park was cleared and traffic moved at an almost normal pace. When I got home from work and we started to fix dinner, Joy kept going to the window, often with a half-opened can or mixing spoon in her hand.

Then a shriek: "Paul, Paul, look! Paul!"

A mugging? An accident? A whole list of misfortunes flashed through my mind as I raced to the window.

"He's there! He made it!"

In the yellowish glare of the street light on the corner, Joy's dog stood atop a mound of plowed snow, calmly surveying his snow-covered territory.

"He's probably starved," Joy said, scooping some of the spaghetti and meatballs we were having for dinner into a tin can.

The dog stayed on his perch until he saw Joy coming across the street toward him. I opened the window and could hear her faintly calling, "Good dog, here's some food; have some food." As she began to cross the street he leaped off the mound and bounded through and over the snow into the darkened park. Joy waited for a few minutes, calling to the dog and extending her hand. Finally she emptied the food onto the top of the mound. Then she turned and walked back to the building.

She dropped the can into the garbage bag without a word. And when we sat down to eat she just pushed her food around the plate. But she said nothing about the dog. She guessed I probably didn't want to hear about him.

Later that night while we both were reading Joy kept on going to the window. About 10:30 she stayed there for quite a while, and I wondered what was going through her mind. She stared out the window, not saying a word.

"Paul, Paul, look!"

It was that excited tone of voice again, the one that tripped a switch inside me that signaled disaster. I ran to the window.

"That little devil," she said, smiling.

"What? What little devil?" I asked, looking out.

"You know what? He waits for a car to pull up and park and the owner to lock up. Then he burrows underneath the front where the engine is. The heat must keep him warm."

We maintained the watch for the next two hours, and sure enough, when a car would pull up nearby, the dog would leave his old spot and crawl beneath the new arrival. He did it three times in the two hours.

As we slipped into our warm bed that night, the last thing Joy said was, "I just hope a lot of people come home late tonight. And I hope they come home about an hour apart."

In the next few weeks, whenever Joy saw the dog, she would take things out for him to eat. Not only would he run away when she came close, he wouldn't even eat the food after she had left.

"Paul, I got so close to him today." Joy came in one day, beaming. "His face, oh, what a face! There's so much sadness and pain and pride in that face. And he's so skinny."

"Remember, just a dog, Joy."

I don't think she heard me.

"There's a thin streak in the middle of his forehead, and one of his ears—the left one—has a white spot on it. He looks right at you with those soft brown eyes like he wants to trust you but can't be sure. He's a beautiful chestnut color on top; it looks like black from up here. And he eats acorns, Paul."

"Remember, just a squirrel, Joy."

"Honest, I watched him. He cracks them open in his mouth, spits out the whole business and then picks the meat out."

As we watched the dog we saw how he did get a more balanced diet. Our apartment had a modern incinerator that burned all the leavings into ashes, but the smaller apartment houses and the row houses did nothing to their garbage before it went into the battered cans. Much of the time these cans would be overflowing, and the dog would pick among the paper bags and bottles to find his food. On a good day there would be pork-chop bones, half a loaf of stale bread, or gobs of mashed potatoes; on a poor day, frosted lettuce leaves or soggy breakfast cereal, both of which he ate very slowly. Obviously, they were not to his liking.

"But he makes it. He's so darn proud," Joy said. "There he is, ribs sticking out, and when I offer him food he runs away. And then he has to pick in the garbage cans. And he's so smart. In that rain yesterday he knew which way the wind was blowing and he got on the right side of the stone wall. And I've seen him during bad weather in the tunnel when I drive across town through the park. He knows where to find his shelter and his food."

"Uuuummm," was my usual enthusiastic response.

During those hard winter months he did have one regular eating place, and we joked about his ethnic origins. The wild dog often waited at the edge of the park until the Italian at the corner pizza store came out to empty his garbage into the can. No sooner would the twisted little man, who had only three teeth—all on the bottom, which produced a strange and wonderful smile—step back into his store than the dog would cross the street. His favorite scraps, Joy observed, were pizzas with sausage.

"Pepperoni must be too spicy because he won't touch it, and green peppers are out," Joy said. "After eating he goes right back to the park, finds a mound of clean snow that hasn't been tracked over and eats the snow to wash it all down. Then he burrows into the mound with his mouth to get cleaned off. What a dog! Continental tastes and manners to match!"

"Uuummmm," I replied.

That winter was a temperamental one. Inches of snow would be followed by temperatures near zero that glazed the entire park in a dirty white frosting. Then we'd have temperatures in the 40's and, except for the huge drifts, the snow would be gone. With the changes in temperature, we managed to have runny noses almost constantly for three months, and many of our friends spent weeks in bed from colds and the flu. The dog somehow managed as the thermometer dipped and rose. We wouldn't see him for days in the coldest weather, and then he'd show up. Each time to Joy it was as if he had been miraculously rescued from certain death. We never knew if he caught a cold—or, in fact, if dogs get colds—but he never seemed to drag around during an unpredictable winter that subdued the human race in New York City.

Chapter Two

W<small>E SAW</small> even more of the dog when spring came to Central Park. The browned grass started to turn green and the daffodils blossomed, popping through the soil that had held them frozen all winter. Growing things have a wonderful way of thumbing their noses at winter. And so did the dog.

He was friskier than ever. He had a special place for a game by one of the drives that went through the park. Alongside the drive was a long wide stretch of grass. As cars wound around the curving drive he would bark out a challenge and chase them on his grassy track until they were stopped by one of the red lights. Then, with a toss of his head, he would go back to the starting point. He had stopped the cars—and he was ready for the next set of contenders.

By spring he had learned more of the city's ways.

No longer did he have to dart across the street, dodging traffic as he went. By spring he waited patiently, right at the crosswalk, for the light to change before he trotted slowly across.

With the luscious spring dews he took a shower a few times a week. In the morning he would rub up against the buds and growing leaves on the bushes or roll over and over down one of the gentle slopes. Then, with a series of violent shakes, he would get rid of most of the water. He would then spend hours licking himself in an effort to shed his coat of the winter's gray.

Joy had watched him make it through the cold, uncertain days of winter to the more promising spring. But all the while, one thing didn't change. He wouldn't let Joy or any other human being near him, even though they offered food.

There were others who wanted to befriend him, feed him. They, like us, had watched his struggle to survive the winter. An old lady from our building who needed two canes to walk, firemen from the firehouse just around the corner, a telephone repairman who regularly worked inside apartments on our block—they all tried to give him food, but he would have none of their charity.

Often, when dog owners would take the collars off their dogs in the park, the wild dog would run and frolic with their pets. But if the owner approached, he would always move away. For some reason, he had grown to distrust people. Maybe he had been abandoned in the park by a human he thought he could trust. Those puppy days were not far behind, because as Joy watched him she had noticed that he grew ever so slightly. He had come to full growth—probably celebrating his first birthday—in the brutal winter of Central Park.

But he made it to spring—and spring brought people to the park, and people brought food.

The grown men and the young boys started to play baseball on the open fields. They brought luscious sausages embedded in hero sandwiches and cherry soda and beer. Other young couples came to sit on the grass, to watch the baseball games or just look at the flowers and sky. They brought French fries and ham and cheese sandwiches. Their children brought cookies and Crackerjack. Older couples who sat on the benches brought pastrami and corned beef sandwiches and paper cups full of potato salad.

From one of his resting places the dog would watch the people in the park. Some just left their papers and uneaten food where they sat. In the eyes of many people they were litter bugs. To the wild dog they were considerate. When the sun went down and most of the people left, he would come out.

Pastrami, sausage, cheese. It was as if he were a sophisticated New Yorker, with New York tastes, walking through a cafeteria line. If he didn't find the food he wanted right there he could find it elsewhere in his territory.

Late one afternoon when Joy and I were playing Frisbee we watched him start at the bottom of one trash basket and sniff his way to the top. He inspected a few more baskets before he found one that held food he wanted. He stood up on his back legs, tipped the basket over and proceeded to eat what he had picked out.

As a young male dog on the run in the park he might have been expected to have his girl friends. He did. But again, the wild dog showed a sense far beyond his age or his training, whatever that might have been. Female puppies would tug at their leashes to get away to go to the wild dog. When an owner gave in and let the young pups run free, they would go straight to the wild dog, which would be resting on his haunches. He would have little of the affections of these young ones. He might get up, give them a sniff or two, perhaps circle them once and even slowly wag his tail. But he never followed through. He would quickly be off, bounding across the grass or into a thicket. He was a bachelor on the run but he would not take advantage of a young lady new to the park. Only with the older female dogs would he run and play, his tail straight in the air, his chest puffed out. For a wild dog, he had a sense of what was proper and what was not.

One female the wild dog liked especially was named Checkers. Checkers, a finely groomed black Scottie, was walked by her master every morning at eight and each night about dinnertime. The wild dog seemed to wait for Checkers to make her visits to the park. As Checkers and her master crossed the street and began to walk down the path into the park, the dog would come out of the bushes. He was never so bold as to run up to Checkers. Instead he followed her at a distance of twenty or thirty feet. If Checkers stopped, the dog stopped. When she started up again, so did the dog.

Checkers was never let off the leash, so the dog never got to play with her. He would never go to a dog on a leash. That leash was a link to a human being.

Checkers' master was a retired insurance salesman who lived in our apartment building. On one of his walks with his dog he met another retired resident of the building, an old man who had come from Czechoslovakia some years ago.

"I've watched you with your dog from my window," the Czech said in his heavy accent, "and I've noticed you have a follower, the brown-and-white fellow."

"Yes," the other man said, "but you know how wild dogs are. They run in packs; they're killers, dangerous. That dog could have fleas or rabies or other diseases. I don't want Checkers to catch anything from him."

By this time the two men were sitting on one of the green wooden benches by a playground near the edge of the park. In the distance, shaded by a pink flowering bush, was the wild dog. He was licking mud off his paws. It had rained the night before. Checkers sat at her master's feet, tail wagging slowly, her eyes on the other dog.

The Czech looked over at the wild dog. The old man had sharp, striking features that had made me remember his face from the first time I saw him in the building. He had leathery skin and a startling white crew cut but soft blue eyes. For some reason his face hinted that his life had seen its share of suffering. Just looking at him I often wondered what his boyhood was like and how he lived in his native land before he came to America.

"The dog looks like a fine person to me," he said.

"I wouldn't trust him," the other man warned.

"Yes, yes, I know," the Czech replied, his eyes still on the dog.

It was in late April or early May that we began to see the old Czech making his trips to the park near where the dog usually roamed. He had purchased some dog biscuits and, with the box under his arm, he slowly walked toward where the dog was sitting. The dog would look from side to side as if he didn't even notice the man coming. We could hear the man calling softly to the dog in his native language. Step by step, his words so soothing, he walked toward the dog. And each time, at a certain point, as if some line had been crossed, the dog would bolt away, going deeper into the park.

And each day the man would leave a biscuit on a rock near where the dog had been lying.

After watching this ritual for two weeks, we wondered what success the old man was having. We walked into the park and to the spot where the dog could usually be found. On one rock was a biscuit soaked with the rain and crawling with ants. On another rock a heap of fine tan powder, the remnants of another biscuit. On still another rock, two fresh biscuits—untouched.

"Poor guy," Joy said. "He must see the dog isn't accepting his gifts, yet he keeps coming back."

"The dog's doing okay," I said. "He doesn't need people, I guess. Say, we've got that chicken in the oven and the folks will be here in a half hour. Let's stop worrying about dog biscuits."

We had relatives with us for dinner that night, Joy's sister Shirley and her husband, Cecil, who were visiting from California. As we ate, I tried to turn the conversation to some good movies we'd seen or a book that had been favorably reviewed. But Joy went on about the dog, and it was obvious our guests were more interested in the survival of this wild dog than in talk about the latest of anything.

"He won't take food from a soul," Joy said, "but he eats like a prince out there. A bit messy at times with the trash cans, but not that messy."

"How long have you been watching him?" Shirley asked.

"When was it, Paul? December, right?"

"December?" Shirley said. "And what happened during the winter? Gosh, this isn't exactly Anaheim."

Joy told in vivid detail about his warm resting places beneath parked cars, his rummaging through garbage cans, his intrepid crossing of the busy street next to the park, his games with the cabs and buses and cars.

"But most of the time he just sits over there on a knoll, surveying his kingdom," Joy said, getting up from the table and going to the window. "There he is!" she said.

Chairs scraped against the floor as our relatives scrambled toward the window. And there he was, lazily rolling on his back, getting the last rays of sunshine on his belly.

Shirley watched him, a sad look on her face. She, like her sister, had grown up on a farm and had a great love for animals. Her back yard in Anaheim was a sanctuary for lost dogs. The last dog she had taken in, a big mixed breed they called Moose, had devastated the yard, tearing the lawn to shreds, digging huge holes, uprooting bushes, until her husband had been ready to call the ASPCA. However, Shirley's love for the dog had won. But their back yard isn't what it used to be.

"He'll never make it; the city will get him someday soon," Shirley said. "I'm afraid even to walk in the park, and he lives there. And with nobody to feed him. He'll never make it."

"He's got to," Joy said, trying to sound cheery. "This old man is taking an interest in him. He's trying to give him food."

"He doesn't accept it?" Cecil asked.

"No," Joy said. "He won't take anything offered by humans. He doesn't trust anybody. We'd take him in in a minute if we could."

"Like the lease reads, Joy," I said, "no pets, and that includes wolf dogs."

I found myself laughing alone at my joke. Shirley and Cecil and Joy had their eyes on the dog.

"C'mon, the chicken's getting cold," I said.

Later in the evening, as we were returning from walking our relatives to the subway stop, we ran into the old Czech coming from the Puerto Rican bodega with a quart of milk.

"We've been watching you with the dog," my wife said.

He blinked at first, not knowing us or understanding immediately what my wife was talking about. Then he smiled. "Oh, him. My little wild friend. Not very trusting, is he?"

"I've tried to feed him too, but he just won't take anything from people."

"Too proud?" the old man said.

"Too scared, I think," Joy replied. "He really must have had some bad experiences to make him that afraid."

"Well, tomorrow I'm going to try something new. Someone told me that dogs love chicken livers and hearts. I'm going to boil some for him."

"We've tried everything from spaghetti to steak."

"Chicken livers and hearts. Tomorrow afternoon about five," he said.

"Good, I'll be back from school then; I'll be watching."

Chapter Three

I LEFT WORK early the next day, so both Joy and I were at the window well before five to watch the old man. The dog was in his usual place on the knoll, dozing with his head on his paws.

We saw his head jerk up, and we looked down the path for the old man. But it was still fifteen minutes to five. Suddenly the dog stood up and ran into the park. A group of young boys were playing catch nearby, and their ball had landed near him so he was off.

At five o'clock we could see the old man, with a plastic bag in his hand, crossing the street next to the park. He looked toward the spot where the dog usually could be found but he saw what we did: a gentle rise, some flowering bushes, a huge rock—and no dog. The old man picked up a handful of grass and threw it into the air. He was checking what direction the wind was coming from. When the grass blew directly toward where the dog usually sat, the old man found the nearest bench, sat down and waited.

In a few minutes, the dog appeared. He must have come from the back of the small hill because none of us saw him coming. Even the old man did a double take when he saw the dog standing fifty yards away from him.

The old man walked slowly toward the dog, talking to him in Czechoslovak. We couldn't make out any more than the tone. It sounded as if he were a grandfather holding an ice cream cone, trying to win back the favor of a grandchild he had somehow frightened or offended. The man stopped short of the rocks where he had left the dog biscuits and opened the plastic bag. He knew that if he went much farther the dog would run away.

He tore the bag down one seam and held up its contents so that the wind would take the smell to the dog. There was a mild breeze that day and we couldn't tell if the dog caught the scent or not. He constantly sniffed the air when humans approached him, and he was doing that now.

The old man held the food in the air until his arm wobbled. He rested for a few minutes and held it up again. Then, without a word, he laid the plastic bag on a rock, spread the contents out, turned and walked back to the bench to see if the chicken hearts and livers would do what spaghetti, steak and dog biscuits had failed to do. He watched the dog. We watched too.

The dog sniffed the air again and took two steps in

the direction of the food. Then he sat down and began licking his paws.

"Go on, dog, get it," Joy said quietly, as if she were afraid the dog would be frightened by the sound of her voice—all the way from the fourth-floor window.

But the dog just sat there, looking around, occasionally fixing his gaze on the old man, who sat motionless on the bench.

The man waited an hour; the dog did not move. So the man turned and walked toward the entrance to the park. He was halfway there when Joy grabbed my arm. "Look, Paul, the dog's moving."

The dog came down off his hill. He appeared to be headed back into the park. But then he began to make a wide semicircle and at last was headed toward the food. We looked down and saw that the man had stopped just inside the park and was standing in the shadow of a tree, watching.

The dog arrived at the food and for a few minutes looked all about him. Then, slowly, he took the first piece of meat—it looked like a liver—and began eating. Slowly, carefully, he worked his way through the entire meal. He was in no hurry to finish, although a dog like that, with well-defined ribs, might be expected to be more eager. Once he was finished, he licked the plastic bag and went back to the hill, where he ran his face along the grass to clean up. Then he sat back, licked his jaws and rested his head comfortably on his paws. A nap was in order after that fine meal.

The old man hustled across the street toward the

apartment building. Even from the fourth floor we could see the smile on his face.

Later we learned that when the old man got back to his apartment his wife noticed the smile. He told her about the wild dog accepting the first meal and how he was now sure he could tame him.

"And I have just thought of a name for the dog," he told his wife. "It is a marvelous word from the Hungarian. The Americans will pronounce it—let's see—they'll pronounce it Fitzgo. I name this dog Fitzgo. It is a wonderful name because it means the many things that the dog is. It means a young fellow, well educated, very polite, kind and courteous, but who likes to be a bum. Like a playboy of the park, out for a good time, but a person who would never hurt anyone. Fitzgo!"

Once the dog had accepted the old man's offering of chicken livers and hearts, the man brought him the same delicacies every day for the next week. And each day the dog would eat them after the man had left. Then the man tested his good luck; he brought dog biscuits, leftover meat, bread.

The first time the menu was altered the dog sniffed awhile at the dog biscuits. Then he proceeded to eat them. With each change, the dog took less time to approve the menu. Once the man was far enough away the dog would go to the food and begin to eat.

We don't know if we saw it the first time it happened (we couldn't watch the dog eat every day), but at feeding time the old man began to sit on a green bench outside the apartment, across the street from the park, and put down the food—it was chicken livers and hearts this particular day—on the grass some twenty feet away from his bench.

We waited and watched for about five minutes, but then we saw the wild dog peeking out from behind the stone wall on the edge of the park. He waited for the light to turn green and then trotted toward his food. The man didn't move. The dog went to the food and slowly began to eat. When he was finished he got up quickly and ran back across the street to the park and disappeared behind the stone wall.

"Paul, Paul, the dog's beginning to trust somebody," Joy said ecstatically.

Even I had to agree. "And the old man has made friends with another refugee."

The next time Joy saw the old man, she told him that she had seen the dog come across the street to eat. "And by the way," she said, "I'd appreciate it if you'd kind of keep us posted on how you're doing with the dog. We miss a lot during the day."

The old man smiled. "Of course, of course I will."

After that whenever Joy would see him she'd get the latest on the wild dog and then tell me what had happened. At that time I was researching and writing articles for magazines, and asking questions, getting facts, was not hard for me to do. But this dog was Joy's interest, not mine. She proved to be a good reporter. Several times a week I'd be filled in on the dog's activities with enough details so that, if the interest had been there, I could have written an article about him—or even started a book.

Chapter Four

THE OLD MAN continued to take the wild dog, Fitzgo,
different leftovers. Each day at five o'clock he would put
out the food and wait for the dog to come. But each day
he put the food closer and closer to his bench. Each day
the dog would come out from the park, sniff the air, trot
across the street, eat and then leave. Knowing how dis-
trustful of humans the dog was, the old man never tried
to reach out or touch him.

One day, he took an aluminum piepan, filled it with
warm milk and gave it to the dog. As Fitzgo lapped up
the milk, the man could see that the dog liked it better
than anything—better than anything except chicken livers and hearts, perhaps—he had brought him so far.
When the dog finished, he turned his face toward the
man for just an instant. Little drops of the milk trembled
on his whiskers.

"He was telling me thank you," the man told Joy later. But he told no one else. Who else would have understood that look?

The day after he brought warm milk for the dog, the old man came down to the bench at the usual time, this time with not much to offer: some stale slices of bread. To his amazement the dog was waiting for him, resting, with his paws crossed in front of him, under a nearby tree.

The man was so excited to see that the dog had come to meet him that he dropped the six slices of dry bread and ran back into the apartment. He passed Checkers and her master in the lobby.

"Sorry, no time to talk now, big things are happening," he called to his friend as he ran for the elevator.

He was out of breath when he got to the apartment. He went straight for the cabinet beneath the sink and began to dig through the garbage bag.

"That pie tin I used yesterday, where is . . . ? Oh, here it is," he said to his wife, who didn't know what had happened. He didn't take time to warm the milk. He just tucked the milk container and the piepan under his arm and headed back to the elevator.

The dog was just finishing his last slice of bread when the man got back to his bench. He filled the pan with milk and laid it right at his feet.

To his even greater amazement, once the dog had finished the bread he walked over and began to lap up the milk. It was as if it were the most normal thing to do: follow a dry snack with milk.

The man could hardly wait to tell Checkers' master and his wife.

"He trusts me, this dog," he said to Checkers' master.

"I wouldn't get too friendly with him," the other man responded. "Don't forget that business about biting the hand that feeds you. He's wild. You don't know what might set him off."

"Just be careful, my dear," his wife warned.

But the old man couldn't be worried by them. The next day he brought a feast for the dog, something to celebrate with: an entire pound—a dozen in all—of hot dogs.

He sat on the bench for nearly an hour, from five until six o'clock. The sun was already low in the sky and the long shadows of the trees crisscrossed the grassy areas and the cement playgrounds. He sat patiently, hoping.

Just after six, from around the stone wall, the dog finally came. He looked suspiciously all around him, then walked slowly toward the bench where the man was sitting. The man had spread the feast out at his feet on a clean piece of waxed paper he had brought from his apartment. There the hot dogs sat, six rows, two in each row.

The wild dog started to eat the hot dogs, one at a time. The neat rows were whittled away as he worked his way through them. Halfway through number ten the dog had had enough. He simply dropped the uneaten half of the tenth hot dog on the waxed paper and trotted back to the park, licking the fragments from his jaws.

The man wanted again to tell someone besides Joy about the dog, about how neat and mannerly he was. But he felt sheepish because he thought most people wouldn't care. He wasn't aware that a number of people in the apartment building had watched the dog throughout the winter and spring. He knew my wife and I were following his progress in trying to tame the dog, but he had no idea—nor did we—that dozens of others were cheering him on from the windows of the building.

The next day, on his way back from the post office, he bought a half pound of lean, red ground beef and took it to the spot in the middle of the morning. He sat on the bench and whistled softly to himself as he waited for the familiar brown-and-white face to appear from behind the stone wall.

He began to read his New York Times, and when he got to the second front page a small headline caught his eye—"A.S.P.C.A. Takes Wild Dog Chase." The story told about the wild dogs who roamed the city, the fear people had of them and how the dogs were periodically rounded up. A photograph showed a man pulling a Doberman, and the caption read, "Stray dog caught in Central Park, being put in van."

Reading further into the story, he was encouraged to find that the dog catchers had the roughest time capturing dogs in the park, because they had so much area to escape to without being cornered, as they could be in city streets and alleys. Then the sentence: "Sick, injured and unwanted dogs are disposed of in a high-altitude type of decompression chamber." The old man stopped whistling.

At lunchtime he walked back to the apartment building; Fitzgo had not come. Three or four times during the afternoon he went back to the bench. But still the dog did not come. All sorts of things went through the man's mind. The dogcatcher had gotten Fitzgo; Fitzgo had been run over chasing cars in the park; he had been poisoned by some dog hater.

No, he said to himself, it is only because it is not Fitzgo's dinnertime. He will come then.

The man returned to the bench at five o'clock and waited again. The sun was going down and the street lights were beginning to blink on before he decided to go inside. His shoulders sagging, he picked up the once-red ground meat, which had been dried out and turned brown by the sun and wind, and dropped it into a garbage can. Despondent, he went upstairs and turned on the television set that he couldn't really watch.

The old man had a tough time sleeping that night. His dreams—and the hours he lay awake beside his sleeping wife—were filled with thoughts about the dog. Everything had been going so well. What could have happened? Were the hot dogs spoiled and had they made the dog sick? For some reason he was afraid he would never see the dog again.

The next morning the old man was sitting on the

bench near the apartment, looking listlessly toward the park, when Checkers and her master came by.

"My friend, you look like you haven't been to bed. If you'll excuse me for saying it, you haven't even shaved this morning. What is wrong?"

"The dog," is all the old man could answer. He did not even raise his eyes to meet the other man's look.

His friend just stood there, silent.

"I waited all day yesterday for the dog. I had this nice ground beef for him and he didn't come. I am very worried about him."

"Come with me while I walk Checkers and maybe you'll see the dog."

"No, I just feel too tired to do that. I'll wait here for him."

The Czech was sitting there fifteen minutes later when his friend came puffing across the street from the park. He was having so much trouble breathing that he could only get out a few words at a time. "Under a bush . . . lying there . . . looks like blood . . . green bush with . . . yellow flowers . . . bush and . . . blood."

The old man leaped to his feet. Immediately he sensed what his friend was talking about. "But where, where is he?" he asked, clutching the other man's arm.

"Near the pond . . . in back of the ball field."

A yellow cab screeched to a stop as the old man bolted out into the street, with no thought of the color of the light. "Good way to get killed, Grandpa!" the cabbie yelled, but the old man didn't hear. He was headed for a green bush with yellow flowers.

He half ran, half walked across the park toward the ball field. When he first saw the bush and the dog beneath he thought he had come too late, but as he drew closer he saw a spark of life in the dog's eyes—rather, in the one eye that wasn't swollen shut.

He could hardly believe what he saw. He could not believe anyone could hate an animal so much. There were bloody spots in the dog's fur starting from a slash across his nose to big red blotches that almost covered his tail. His belly and flanks were cleaner; those were places he could reach to lick. But the rest of his body was caked with dirt and blood.

The old man walked slowly toward the dog. As he got closer to him, the dog began painfully to crawl away along the edge of the bush. The old man knew he could catch the wounded dog, but that would do little good. The animal was obviously more frightened of people than he had been before.

He went back to his apartment and warmed some leftover stew meat and some potatoes. On his way through the lobby the elderly lady who walked with the two canes stopped him. "I hope that's going for the dog. That was terrible."

Surprised by her words, the old man asked how she knew about the dog. "I've watched you feed him in the park—I tried to do the same thing but he would never take food from me. Then I watched you feed him by the bench. It was one of the treats of my day. But then those kids yesterday went after him. And I didn't know who to call. If I called the police, they would maybe call the dogcatcher."

"Who? Who did it to the dog?" the old man asked, his voice growing louder.

"A bunch of boys. Some of them had sticks. Some of them threw cans and rocks at the dog. There must have been ten of them, and every place the dog went they followed. It was terrible. Like a pack of wolves they were. But I didn't know who to call. And that poor dog, he never once barked at them. I wished he could have bit every one—hard!"

"If it ever happens again, let me know," the old man said, and he told the old woman his apartment number. With that, he was out of the building and hurrying back to the dog.

He stopped at the edge of the bushes where the dog could see him and carefully put the leftovers on a grassy, shaded spot. Then he walked away and leaned against a tree a hundred yards from the dog and watched. At first there was no movement from the dog. Then, slowly, painfully, Fitzgo slid on his belly toward the food.

For over a week the old man took food and milk to the dog, and after a few days he could see that the dog was getting stronger. Yet every time he tried to come closer to the dog, he would move away. Now the dog was able to get up and walk to the food, and his fur showed little of the dirt and blood it had been covered with a week before.

The old man went about feeding the dog without

telling anyone, not even his wife. His wife was younger than he and worked during the day. She always cooked a big dinner at night so he could have the leftovers for lunch. During those days the leftovers went to Fitzgo and the old man had cheese sandwiches and soup.

One sunny day, late in spring, he was ready to cross into the park to feed the dog. He looked to see if there were any cars coming, and his eye caught a familiar white-and-brown object.

There was Fitzgo, sitting under a tree near the bench, in his old place, waiting for his food. It was the first time in ten days that he had been out of his shelter in the park.

Now that the dog was better, the old Czech made two trips a day to the bench. Fitzgo was always waiting for him when he arrived with his pan of soup or some special food from his native land, such as ground beef wrapped in cabbage leaves or blood sausage. With each day the man began the slow process of putting the food closer and closer to his bench before he sat down.

Finally the day came when the old man sat down first and then laid the food at his feet. It was a wonderful meal that day—chunks of lamb in a rich gravy. The dog didn't seem to mind that this human was a foot away from the food; he walked right up to the dish. As the dog began to eat, the old man extended his hand, slowly, until he touched the dog's back.

It was as if someone had struck the dog. He jumped at the old man's touch and ran across the street, stopping at the stone wall. There he cowered, looking fearfully at the man.

The old man was saddened; he had frightened his little friend. After a while he extended his hand to show the dog he didn't want to harm him. Finally the dog stopped shaking, but he would not move from the wall.

The next day, the old man brought warmed milk with chunks of Italian bread floating in it. The dog, who was sitting under the tree, saw him coming and began to walk slowly toward the bench. The man moved very slowly, so as not to scare the dog. The dog kept coming, and so did the man. They reached the bench at the same time.

The man kept the warmed milk and bread on the bench for a moment. He dipped three fingers into the milk and slowly extended his hand. At first the dog backed off. The man held his hand still. Fitzgo, the wild dog of Central Park, looked the man in the eyes, looked at the hand, looked over at the pan of food, looked back at his eyes. Then he took three small steps forward and sniffed the man's hand.

The old man was so happy he had trouble keeping his hand from shaking. Still, the dog continued to sniff. The man slowly took back his hand and placed the warm meal at his feet.

Eagerly, the dog began to eat, taking the now spongy pieces of bread into his mouth and squeezing the milk into the pan. When the bread was finished, he neatly lapped up the warm milk.

As the man looked down on the dog, he could see that some scars would remain from the horrible day when the boys had chased and beaten him. On his nose, where there had been a spot of blood as big as a silver dollar, there was now a mark that looked like a part in a man's hair, thin and straight and clean.

Once the dog had finished his meal, he would usually go back under the tree to clean his mouth with long, lazy sweeps of his tongue. That day, the dog stayed in place near the man and began to clean up.

Without thinking, the old man put out his hand and laid it softly on the dog's head. At first the dog ducked, as if he were going under a branch. But then he straightened up. The man patted his head lightly and then moved his hand along the dog's back. His breath was coming in short huffs, he was so excited. When he reached the base of the dog's tail the man scratched there. And to his surprise, he saw that the dog started to lazily wag his tail.

"That's a good place, my friend; dog's can't get to it by themselves." The voice startled the old man and caused Fitzgo to move away a few feet. It was Checkers' master.

"Checkers loves it back there. It's her favorite spot."

"Then I will scratch my Fitzgo there. Every day," the Czech said, beaming.

Chapter Five

TALL BUILDINGS in any city—some say especially in New York—prevent people from getting to know each other. With people above us, below us and sandwiching us on all sides, we are still surrounded by strangers. People who might live just the thickness of a wall away from you are unknown. People live on the same floor, ride the same elevator day after day, but when the door opens on his floor each person dashes to the privacy of his apartment rather than stand and talk.

Joy and I are normally outgoing people, but our years of apartment living had conditioned us well. Once inside that apartment building, we didn't go out of our way to meet the people who lived so close to us. In our early married years, we liked the privacy that apartment living offered, but that need for privacy was wearing off. We wanted to get out of the sky and down onto the street. We wanted to live in a house.

We were tired of paying rent month after month and having nothing to show for it. Our lease was coming up for renewal, and we knew the management would be asking for another $25 or $30 a month, which would make our already stretched budget even harder to balance. Many couples our age who have lived in city apartments eventually have to buy a house to survive financially, but most can't wait to get out to the suburbs. Joy and I loved the city, so we were determined that we would stay and find a city house. That's why, during the summer and fall months that Fitzgo and the old man became fixtures at the green bench, we were often away looking at houses in the evenings and on week ends.

But Joy, good reporter that she was, was able to keep up to date on Fitzgo by watching him from the window whenever she could and by talking to the old man and the other people who had watched the dog through the months. As it turned out, that bench did an almost impossible thing: it provided a meeting spot for people in our building who hadn't talked to each other before. Gathered around the old man and the wild dog, people seemed to begin to open up. For once, they had a common concern, something that there could only be friendly conversation about—Fitzgo.

"Fine dog you have there," said one middle-aged man who wore small spectacles and who looked like a lawyer. "I remember him during the winter when his ribs showed through his filthy coat. You are taking very good care of him."

Another man, who left early in the day and returned early in the afternoon from his job as captain on the Staten Island ferry, stopped by often. "Holy mackerel, look at the poor dog's paws; if three toes are straight then the other two are broken. He must have had a rough life. If he could tell us, what wild stories they would be."

The Czech nodded. "In a way I'm happy he can't talk. The stories would probably make us all cry. But now he has someone to take care of him. He is a fine dog, isn't he?"

Joy stopped by one day to talk with the old man, to look at Fitzgo. "I brought some leftover steak down; do you think he'll take it now that he's tame?" she asked the old man.

"Tame? No, he was never wild. He just trusts now. Try and see."

Joy put out her hand with the tasty bit of beef in it. "Fitz, Fitzgo, come here, good boy." The dog, which was sitting beside the old man, did not move. Joy moved toward him, her hand extended. "Fitz, good boy; here's some steak for you." She moved closer.

When she was just a few feet from the dog, he got up and moved away. As Joy followed him, he continued to keep a safe distance from her.

"It's no use," she said. "Here, you feed it to him."

"Come, friend, and eat this good meat," the old man said to the dog, and Fitzgo immediately came to him and ate the meat out of his hand.

"I wish he'd believe in me the way he does in you," Joy said, "just that I want to be his friend and feed him."

"You know how long it took for him to trust me. Maybe I will be the only one," the man said, not without pride in his voice, "or someday he might trust others."

"My husband and I watched him and you from the start. We always show Fitzgo to our friends and tell them about how he survived the winter and how you tamed . . . er . . . made friends with him. You know, he's the kind of dog I've always wanted. He has such gentle ways."

"Ah, now he belongs to the park, but I hope someday I can convince him to live with me and my wife," the man said, with determination in his voice.

"I know, you deserve him; you've worked so hard. But even my husband—he thought Fitzgo looked like a wolf—even he has taken more to the dog now. He says he looks like the kind of dog that would curl up at your feet at night and sleep there while you read a book. I guess that's his definition of a good dog. He hates those poodles with their ribbons and rhinestone collars."

"We shall see what Fitzgo decides, if he wants to live inside or out."

"But then there's that business about the lease; how could you work that out?"

"Are you kidding?" The old man smiled. "With so many people loving Fitzgo, who would report him? And if anyone did, I would tell the management his story and they would let me keep him."

"I'm sure of that," Joy said.

As they got to be better friends, the old man would see the dog many times during the day. At mealtimes, twice a day, the dog would be waiting. But any time during the day that the man got restless or bored inside his apartment, he would whistle out his window. Soon Fitzgo would be seen running past the stone wall toward the bench where he knew the old man would be as fast as the elevator and his legs could take him there.

The summer was upon New York City, and with the warmer days the man spent more time outside with his dog. Young mothers pushing their baby carriages, the postman, the young boys delivering groceries would stop and talk with him. But, for all the people wanting to come close to him, the dog would let no one but the old Czech touch him or feed him.

It was almost as if there was an invisible stick, six feet long, that the dog held out. If people stayed that far away, he was comfortable and would doze in New York's smoggy sunlight. When they came closer, he would move a safe distance away.

After a while the dog began to follow the man back to the building after each visit. He would trot alongside until they came to the door that led to the lobby. When the man went to the door the dog would turn and head for the park.

Soon, the dog was waiting for the man to come out. He stood outside the lobby like some marble statue of a famous and heroic dog, and waited. When he saw the man, his tail would start wagging furiously.

"The dog is now my friend," he told his wife, "and

47

I think it is time we invited my friend to our apartment for a visit."

Before taking him into the apartment building, the man thought he should have the dog on a leash to keep him under control in the lobby and in the elevator. So he went to a variety store on the next block and told the clerk about the dog.

"Only one way to do it," said the clerk with a very sure tone in his voice. "Get a choke chain."

"Choke chain!" replied the man.

"It's very simple, you put this chain around that wild dog's neck and when he tries to run off it'll choke him so quick he'll stop on a—on a dog biscuit," he said, laughing.

"That's terrible. I would never choke my dog Fitzgo. I would never choke a gentleman like him."

"Okay, do as you like. I'll still have the choke chains in stock when you come back."

Later that day, Checkers and his master were walking in the park with Fitzgo and the man as their companions. The man had told Checkers' master what the clerk said about choke chains.

"Maybe he's right," Checkers' master said. "Don't forget, you're not dealing with a show-trained animal. He's still a wild beast."

That hurt the old man, to have his friend called such a thing. "Let us see how wild he is," he said. "Please hold Checkers for a while and lend me her collar and leash."

The man sat down on a park bench and called Fitzgo to him. He patted the dog on the head and then ran his hand down his back, scratching all the way. The dog responded by wagging his tail contentedly. The old man let Fitzgo sniff the leash. The dog, recognizing Checkers' smell, wagged all the more. Then the man carefully placed a loop of the chain around the dog's neck and waited to see what would happen.

Nothing. The dog continued to wag his tail and to look into the old man's eyes. Suddenly, Fitzgo heard a branch crackle behind him; it was one of the city sanitation men walking toward a trash basket he was going to empty. With that jerk of his head, the dog tightened the chain around his neck. His eyes opened wide, as if some terrible memory had been brought back to him in that instant.

He reared back like a frightened horse and made for the sprawling meadow in the center of the park. The collar and hand strap from the chain danced crazily along the ground after him, catching cans and tossing them aside, kicking up handfuls of stones. As the old man watched, the strap caught on the spiny edge of a wire fence at one of the baseball diamonds. "Aaaahh," was the sound the man made, as he grimaced, seeing his friend jerked to a stop. But the dog shook loose and ran over a hillside into a clump of trees and out of sight.

The old man sat, dazed, on the bench and looked at the clump of trees for a few minutes. There was no sign of his friend. It was only when Checkers' master cleared his throat that the old man remembered he wasn't alone.

"The dog might choke himself. Perhaps we should try to find him," the old man said to his friend.

"Maybe you're right," his friend said as he picked up Checkers and headed back toward the apartment. "But you can look for that wild thing yourself. That collar and chain cost ten dollars, and Checkers' rabies shot tag is on it too. If this dog has to get another shot because of that thing running around out there, I won't be too happy about it."

Chapter Six

THE OLD MAN walked through the park until nightfall, looking for the dog. He would have kept on looking, but he knew that no one but the foolhardy walked in that section of the park after dark. He went back to his apartment and told his wife the sad story.

"It would be such a shame if all the time you put into that dog would go to waste and the poor thing would choke to death someplace in that park."

At the word "choke" the old man let out a sigh that could barely be heard. But his wife heard it, and she knew how heavily the dog's fate rested on his mind.

Early the next morning, even before the *New York Times* was delivered or the tiny restaurant across the street had served its first breakfast, the old man was back in the park. The dew on the grass quickly soaked his shoes but he kept on walking, looking and shouting, "Fitzgo, Fitzgo, come here, good dog."

Tennis players walking to their courts looked at this strange man calling to a dog that was nowhere in sight; children giggled to their friends about him. The old man didn't care; he continued to call out until he was almost hoarse. He stopped at noontime at one of the hot dog wagons that are marked by orange and black umbrellas and are usually run by men whose accents tell they are new arrivals to America.

After eating half a hot dog the man continued his search. He stuffed the other half into his pocket—just in case. His voice began to give out, but he did as best he could with what he had left. His eyes scanned the flat, grassy stretches of the park, the rocks, the trees, the hills, the bushes. He was walking along the edge of the road that cuts across the park at 96th Street when he had the feeling he was being followed. In Central Park, even in the daytime, that often is not a good thing. The old man walked faster, but he could feel there was someone behind him keeping pace. He could walk no faster and he didn't want to try to run, so he quickly looked over his shoulder.

There, just ten or fifteen feet behind him, was Fitzgo.

There was no sign of the leash. The dog had his head bent low, and he looked sheepishly at the old man with his soft brown eyes as if he wondered if he would still be welcome. His tail was between his legs, just as it had been during the early days when the man had first seen him.

The old man reached out his hand and said softly,

"Fitzgo, Fitzgo." The tail rose up and wagged slowly at first. Extending his hand, the man said the dog's name again and Fitzgo came to him, his tail wagging faster with each step. He sniffed the old man's hand and then, with a big swipe of his tongue, licked it from the tip of his fingers to his wrist. The old man pulled out the other half of the hot dog, took it out of the bun and gave it to his friend, who swallowed it in three bites.

The old man, with Fitzgo trotting along at his side, walked back through the park, determined to try something. When they reached the street next to the park, the man and dog stood for a few seconds, waiting for the light to change. Then they walked to the apartment building entrance.

It was the middle of the afternoon so there was no one around the entrance. The old man looked through the window and saw that no one was in the lobby, either.

He climbed the two low steps leading to the door, but the dog stayed on the sidewalk as he had always done before. This time, the man called to him and patted his leg, motioning for the dog to come. The dog looked as if he didn't know what to do.

"Fitzgo, Fitzgo," the man called to him again. "Come, come with me." Fitzgo looked at the steps and lowered his tail. Then, suddenly, with a bound, he leaped over the steps and was standing alongside the man, who opened the door. The two of them walked inside.

The lobby of the building had a cold, marblelike floor, and at first the dog had trouble walking. He would slip and then, when he thrust out his front paws to stop, he would slide. Finally he learned that by taking small steps he could control his walk on this strange surface. Then the man knew he faced the biggest challenge of all: getting Fitzgo into an elevator.

The elevator was waiting, its doors open. The old man walked up to it and then walked past. Fitzgo stayed beside him. Just as the man was ready to take Fitzgo on the elevator, another resident of the building came into the lobby with her two poodles. One was black, the other white, and both had pink ribbons behind their ears. They yapped high-pitched barks toward Fitzgo. The dog just stood his ground, his tail now high in the air, his body erect. The man decided to let the elevator go.

When it came back to the lobby floor, the old man was relieved to find no one in it and no one waiting. He calmly stepped inside and motioned to the dog. Fitzgo started toward him, but then the dog's instinct warned him. One glance at the green walls of this cage and Fitzgo stepped back.

"Come, Fitzgo, good dog." The man spoke to the dog reassuringly. "There is nothing to be afraid of. I'm here with you. I would let nothing harm you. Ever. Come, good dog."

The old man dropped to his knees, which made a cracking sound.

"Fitzgo, come, Fitzgo. I want you to visit in my house." Then his voice took on a pleading tone. "You wouldn't refuse my invitation, would you? You are my fine friend."

With the change in voice, the dog took a step forward. Then another. One paw touched down inside the elevator. Then he was inside. The old man touched the button for his floor and the doors closed. Fitzgo had a panicked look as he was closed in. He immediately began to shake. His tail was already between his legs.

As the elevator began its trip, Fitzgo's legs turned soft. He could not sense what was going on, this strange movement that pressed his body down.

The man stayed on his knees and reached out for the dog. And Fitzgo readily allowed the man to hug him until the doors opened on the floor where the man lived. Fitzgo bolted out of the man's arms and out of the elevator. He almost ran into the wall that was only a few feet from the door.

The man smiled down at his frightened little friend and walked toward his apartment. He turned the key in the door and this time there was no convincing needed. Just as though he had lived there all his life, Fitzgo walked into the living room.

"Our friend has come to visit, I see," the man's wife said, getting up from an easy chair where she had been doing some knitting.

The old man stood silently and proudly at the door.

"So, when a guest comes, we feed him, don't we?" she said. "Get that roast pork we have left over from last night and some gravy. Here, let me do it. Gravy is no good when it's cold."

Just about the time Fitzgo was stepping into the old man's apartment, Joy and I were stepping over rotten flooring and fallen plaster in a run-down rooming house just off Broadway on Manhattan's Upper West Side. It was the tenth house we had seen, and by far the worst, and yet the asking price was high, so high that we would have to rent out most of the building to be able to afford to live in a small part of it. And even if we could have managed the monthly payments, we weren't sure the bank would grant us the mortgage.

Joy was working as a counselor at an all-boy's school and had a small but steady income. I was cutting back on the days I would work at a publishing house, so I could spend more time at the work I really wanted to do: writing magazine articles. After having articles published in *New York*, *The New York Times Sunday Magazine* and *The Atlantic*, I was taking my dream job a bit more seriously: becoming a full-time free-lance writer. But that never impressed bank people when we talked about mortgages. They didn't want to hear about my *possible* income.

So, as we shuffled from room to room in a building that looked slated for demolition, depressed and tired and sure that we would never find a house, the old man went happily from door to door on his floor to tell his friends that the wild dog was at last in his apartment. To some of them whom we talked to later he sounded like a proud young father telling of the birth of a child.

Neighbors came by to see Fitzgo: a ballet teacher, a social worker, a music store clerk, an electrical supplies salesman. And there were more; some came from other floors once the word began to spread.

"Aren't you afraid he'll turn on you?" one asked.

"He has never even growled," the old man said proudly.

"What does he eat?" asked another.

"The same as you and I," said the man as he smiled toward his wife. "Roast pork and nice hot gravy."

As all these people filed in and out, Fitzgo paid them no attention and sniffed his way around the room. He smelled legs of tables, the sofa, the rug. Of course the man was worried that the dog might not sense that he was not to do his business in the apartment. Rugs and grass may feel similar, but . . . He watched and waited as the dog sniffed.

When it was time for the couple to go to bed, they wondered what to do with the dog.

"How about the bathroom?" his wife suggested. "He can't do much damage in there."

"No, that won't do," the old man replied. "He'll feel like we're caging him in. He's still not used to being indoors. Let's just spread newspapers all over the floors, and that way he can't do any harm."

In a half hour the entire apartment was a sea of newspapers, not only on the floors but on the furniture. Fitzgo had already found himself a comfortable lair beneath a chair that had a heavy fringe on it. The fringe served as a swinging door, giving the dog complete privacy within. But outside that lair, wherever he stepped during the night, there were newspapers.

The old man had trouble falling asleep; he kept thinking he was hearing the papers rustle.

57

He awoke with a start early the next morning, even before the alarm clock went off, and found himself already sitting upright in bed alongside his sleeping wife. Next to the bed, with his tail wagging, was Fitzgo.

A quick look around the apartment showed the man that the dog had been a perfect gentleman. The newspapers were as clean as they had been the night before.

From that day on, the man would feed the dog early in the morning, about seven o'clock, and then take him outside to run free until about nine, when they would walk to the post office to check his box. Sometimes the dog would come into the apartment after the post office trip and gingerly walk into the elevator. Other times the dog would stay outside, choosing to run free in the park. But whenever the man called from his window or whistled, it was not long before the dog came bounding out of the park, headed toward the bench.

One morning, soon after Fitzgo had been allowed into the apartment, the old man noticed some movement on the dog's back. Lying in the sun in front of a large window that looked downtown toward New York's sky-scrapers, the dog appeared to be sleeping. Yet his back was quivering with motion.

The old man looked closer. And closer. There on the dog's back was a sea of fleas.

Without telling his wife the man, later that morning, went out and bought some flea powder. With the dog at his feet near the bench, he began to sprinkle the powder on his back. The smell must have irritated Fitzgo's nose, because he sneezed several times and began to move away. Luckily the man had brought along the hairbrush that he was using on the dog. And, by brushing a little—which Fitzgo liked—and sprinkling a little—which he did not—the old man was able to get the job done.

When the old man looked at the brush he knew he had another job to do.

On a warm day that week the old man took off all his clothes except his shorts and took Fitzgo into the bathroom. He had already filled the tub about a quarter full of pleasantly warm water. As he lifted the dog off the bathroom tile he could feel him beginning to shake.

"Fitzgo, Fitzgo, I would never hurt you," he said, holding the dog to his chest. "I just want to clean you up."

With that he stepped into the tub and placed the quaking dog in the water. He got down on his knees in the tub and the dog quickly put his head under the man's arm, as if by hiding he could avoid the bath.

As the old man began to run water over the dog's back, he was amazed at what the water brought with it. When the dog had slept under cars for warmth, he rubbed against the greasy undersides. Oily blotches formed in the tub as the water dripped off his back. The cake of white soap turned black in the old man's hands as he scrubbed the dog. Bits of gravel that had been held in place by the oily dirt settled on the tub's bottom. When the old man had finally finished his job, the widest and dirtiest bathtub ring he had ever seen in his life had been left behind—and he had changed the bath water four times.

He took a giant bath towel and began to dry the dog. This Fitzgo liked. He stood perfectly still and let the man rub him dry. Fitzgo had never looked very dirty to the old man, but the dog's dazzling white and chestnut coat surprised him.

When the old man and the dog got on the elevator to go down into the sunshine, a retired schoolteacher who lived on one of the floors above was already inside.

"What are you doing with *that* dog?" she asked. "My friends told me you had taken in the poor thing that used to run around in the park. Whatever happened to him?"

The old man just smiled at her.

"Didn't you hear me?" she asked. "What are you doing . . . ?" She was looking down at Fitzgo, and she never completed the sentence. "Well, I'll be! He's beautiful!" was all she said for the rest of the trip down.

Chapter Seven

O NE SATURDAY MORNING Joy and I came out of our apartment, on our way to take a second look at a brownstone house in the Park Slope section of Brooklyn. The first time around, the only thing that impressed us about the house was its price—low. The house had little personality and wasn't exactly in the area we were hoping for. But after drawing and redrawing potential floor plans and being realistic about how much money would be coming in during the next few years, we began to think the house might work after all.

We hesitated in front of the building that morning and watched the parade of people coming out. Fitzgo was lying by the bench, and over half of the people went out of their way to wish him a good morning, saying hello to the dog as if he were some old friend.

People who saw Fitzgo and the old man walking

into the lobby would often hold the elevator door so they could ride up and find out about the dog's latest doings. And the old man never disappointed them. It seemed Fitzgo was always doing something different.

"He talks to me," the old man would say. "Different barks mean different things, but only I can tell what he is saying." Or, "he knows what floor is ours when we reach it on the elevator, even before I get out." And Fitzgo would stand beside the man proudly, almost as if he knew he was being talked about. Then, on the man's floor, tail wagging, he would follow his master off the elevator.

Many people knew him by name or at least by appearance—that is, except for newcomers. One of these was the new doorman. By the time he took his job in the fall, Fitzgo was in the habit of coming into the lobby without the old man. The dog would come in and wait patiently when the old man was late or when the weather was bad. It was on a rainy day in November that the ballet teacher who lived in the building ran up the stairs and into the building, holding the door open for Fitzgo and a grocery boy who had bags in each arm. The woman was in the little nook where the mailboxes were when she heard the new doorman call gruffly from the back of the lobby to the boy, "Hey, get your mutt outta here."

"Not mine, buddy," the boy said.

"Well, whose is he, then?"

"This is the second time I've been in the building,

buddy. I don't know the people and I sure don't know the dogs."

"Looks like a stray to me. He's going right back where he came from." With that, the man opened the door. "Okay, Rover, let's go. Out."

The woman came back into the lobby and saw Fitzgo looking at the guard and then looking toward the elevator. "Calm down for goodness' sakes; that's Fitzgo," she said, shuffling through her mail.

"Your dog, lady?" the doorman asked, with no note of politeness in his voice.

"No, but . . ."

"He belong to somebody in the building?"

"Yes, the white-haired old man tamed him; he used to run wild in the park."

With that the doorman's eyes narrowed. "This dog on the old man's lease?"

"Well, not exactly; you see, he's rather a . . . a special case." The woman didn't know what to say. The company that ran the building had strict rules about pets, but they never enforced them. The woman also knew that only those pets owned by residents before they moved in and that were listed on the lease could be legally kept.

"Every one's a special case. Now either get him out of here or I will."

"Must you really!" the woman said, angrily stuffing the mail into her purse. "Come on, Fitzgo, I'm afraid you've got to go out now."

63

The dog looked at her, then at the guard, and walked slowly toward the elevator.

"Please, Fitzgo, come with me," she said.

The dog just stared back at her.

"Okay, lady, if you can't move him, I can," the doorman said, opening the custodian's closet. He found a piece of rope and made a small loop in it and came after the dog.

Fitzgo sensed the danger. He tried to run around the man, but the doorman dropped the loop around his neck. Fitzgo's first reaction was to pull away. As had happened with the chain in the park, this just tightened the hold. He reared back but the doorman had a firm hold on the rope. He jerked the rope and, with that, pulled Fitzgo right off his feet and started dragging the dog toward the door.

"You'll kill him!" the woman screamed at the doorman.

He said nothing. He just dragged the kicking and whining dog across the marble floor, opened the door and gave Fitzgo a tremendous yank that shot the dog through the opening, down the two stone steps and onto the sidewalk.

The woman went over to the rows of doorbells and rang the old man's apartment. She rang again, longer this time.

Meanwhile, his work done, the doorman tried to get the rope back. Fitzgo, recovering from his shock, was now on his feet, tugging at the rope, trying to get free. The guard was wary that the dog would bite him if he tried to untie the rope. So he whipped the rope back and forth, hoping it would shake free from the dog's neck. That made it even tighter and added several loops around the dog's neck.

By the time the woman gave up ringing for the old man and got to the street she found at one end of the rope a tired, angry and by now frightened doorman. At the other end was an exhausted, dirty, half-strangled dog.

"Rotten mutt won't let me near him," the doorman gasped. "I just want to get the rope back."

"You'll get it back after you kill the poor thing," she said, angry, yet close to tears. "Stop pulling for a minute and let me see what I can do."

Fitzgo was still tugging with all the strength he had left when the man let the rope fall slack. The dog, caught off balance, stumbled and fell. He lay there, heaving, as the woman came up to him, saying his name softly.

"Fitzgo, don't be afraid. Just let me help you. Don't be scared." The woman was at least as afraid as the dog was, worried how he would react to anyone's touch after such brutality. She could see that the dog's eyes followed her as she came closer to him. Yet he did not move. She laid her hand on his head and moved toward the knotted rope.

When she began to unwind the looser portions of the rope, Fitzgo twitched a few times but otherwise did not move. Up this close, she could see that the rope had cut past the dog's fur and that there was a smudge of blood where the skin had been rubbed raw. She felt the wetness of that blood as she put her finger under the rope to help the dog breathe easier. Finally she was able to work the knot free.

She wanted to throw the rope back at the doorman, to say something nasty to him. But she just dropped the rope and looked down at the dog.

Slowly, painfully, Fitzgo got to his feet. Without a sound he shakily made his way to the patch of grass near the bench.

Late the same afternoon Joy was watering some plants in one of the windows that looked out over the bench. "He's dead, Fitzgo's dead!" she screamed. I came running out to look down with her at the spot where the dog lay motionless. We both stood there without saying a word.

"Wait, I think he moved his head," I said.

"Yes, yes, he's alive; let's go downstairs."

Before we did, Joy got out a small pan, filled it with water and took along some slices of lunch meat.

When we got downstairs we found that a few other people had seen the dog and had come down to see what they could do.

One woman had placed a bag of groceries beside the dog and had poured some milk into a container she must have found nearby. Another man was gently stroking him. Fitzgo was in no shape to resist anyone's touch.

"It looks like he's been poisoned," one man said.

"Maybe he got hit by a car," said another.

"Look at that mark on his neck," said the woman

with the bag of groceries. "Somebody tried to strangle the poor thing."

"You're right," came a low voice from the bench behind them. It was the old man, whom no one had noticed. He had just been sitting there, his hands in his lap, his eyes on the dog.

He told the people—as he had been told—about the doorman's battle with the dog. And he told them how the dog had refused food and water and just lay there for hours. Fitzgo would not even drink or eat from the old man's hand.

"We have to let nature take its course," the man said sadly. "Let's hope; let's pray for the best."

Joy reached down and for the first time touched the dog she had been watching for almost a year. Fitzgo just looked up at her and blinked and then closed his eyes.

"He won't die, will he?" Joy asked, directing her question to no one in particular. "After everything he's lived through, it can't end like this." I could tell she was fighting back tears.

"Let's hope; let's pray for the best," the old man repeated.

The other people started to go away, but the old man stayed there with his friend. We went back upstairs, but every fifteen minutes or so Joy would look out to see what if anything had happened. All she saw was a dog and a man, both very still.

Near nightfall, the man got up and went over to the dog and gently patted him. The dog raised his head and tried to get to his feet, but at first he was too weak.

Finally he managed to get on all four shaky paws, but he couldn't move without stumbling.

The old man bent over and gently picked up the dog, cradling him in his arms. It was like a slow-motion movie, this old man and his injured dog, making their way to the lobby door.

The old man took care of the dog as if Fitzgo were a member of the family. He bathed the wound on the dog's neck several times and then, when the dog was willing to eat, he started him on warm milk. It was soothing for Fitzgo's throat, which was sore and swollen. From milk the old man went to beef bouillon, then to heavier soup, and then finely diced pieces of meat.

"He's getting better now," the old man told Joy in the lobby a few days after the incident. "He sleeps a lot during the day by the radiator, but he is now able to walk more strongly. Soon he can go back into the park. He misses that. There is still that blood in him."

A few days later, Fitzgo and the old man were outside again. Fitzgo was not his frisky old self yet, but he kept pace with the man as he walked through the park. When a squirrel would catch the dog's eye, he would dash a few yards in that direction but quickly slow to a walk. Then he'd return to the old man's side.

As Fitzgo grew healthier and ready to live a normal life, divided between time in the old man's apartment and time free in the park, none of us knew that other events were being set in motion that would affect the lives of many people in the building. It's hard to figure out exactly why the management decided to crack down.

Maybe the incident with Fitzgo angered the door-man or maybe he was hurt by the icy silence he received from people in the building. Maybe he told his bosses about the dog and explained that he was just trying to do his job. Whatever the real cause, they began to enforce the "fine print" of the leases that they had not bothered with before.

We were not the only people on our floor to re-ceive a sternly worded letter that we were "harboring a dishwasher, clothes washer, clothes dryer or any other unauthorized appliance" and that we would be evicted unless it was removed. Yes, we did have a portable dishwasher, but so did several other people we knew in the building. We were surprised by the letter but when we went to the section of our lease that the letter referred to, sure enough, it didn't allow dishwashers.

It would only be a few weeks until we moved to the house in Brooklyn, so we just tucked the dishwasher in the back of one of the closets, covered it with blankets and hung long winter coats in front of it.

We were at the apartment very little in December because all our spare time was spent demolishing the in-terior of our house in Brooklyn. That was the first step in the renovation that we planned. Old walls had to be taken down, old appliances carted out, rotten flooring torn up. So when we came back to the apartment late at night with our clothes covered with plaster dust and dirt, there wasn't much time to check on Fitzgo—let alone find out what was going on in the building.

Had we been there more of the time, we would have found out about another set of mimeographed notices that went to certain residents, telling them that they were "harboring a pet or other animal not specified in the lease agreement". The old man found one of these notices in his mailbox.

He knew what his lease said about pets. But he also felt that Fitzgo was more than a personal pet; he was a special case. "An idle threat," he said. "This says they will evict me if I don't get rid of this 'illegal pet.' They would never do that. They would never make me get rid of Fitzgo. The people of the building would be up in arms about it."

A week later, the old man found a certified letter in his box at the post office. He quickly opened it. At the top in large letters was written NOTICE OF EVICTION and the last words were "if not complied with within ten days, the order of eviction will be final."

The man's first reaction was to tear the letter up. Instead, he stood in the lobby and showed it to some of the people who knew Fitzgo's background.

"We must do something," the old man said. "We must put pressure on the management in some way so that Fitzgo can stay. He is my dog, yes, but he is also the dog—the spirit, the mascot—of this building. He brought us all together. I would not know many others if it were not for Fitzgo. He gave us a chance to talk to one another."

All of the people were angry about the eviction notice, but their answers did little for the old man.

"What can we do against the management? If we protest, we'll get evicted too," the electrical supply salesman said.

"New York apartments are murder to come by; I don't want to lose mine," the music store clerk said, quickly adding, "but don't get me wrong; I'd do anything for that dog. I love him as much as you do."

"Somebody complained last year and when their lease came up for renewal, the management found something nitpicking wrong and wouldn't let them renew," said the lady who walked with two canes.

It was past the dinner hour and the old man was tired of making his plea. The social worker, a young man in his mid-twenties, came into the lobby, and the old man tried once again to convince someone to help him.

"Have them write letters," the social worker said. "That's the only way. Or make phone calls to the management. But letters are best. If they got a flood of letters, they'd have to make an exception."

The old man spent the next day and evening in the lobby or on different floors in the building, talking to people. Fitzgo stood by his side as he pleaded with them to help. Some said they were sorry but they really didn't want to get involved. Others said they would like to help, but was it worth it for just one dog? Others said they would write or call, but the lack of determination in their voices told the old man they probably would not follow through.

The old man slumped into his chair that night and told his wife about talking to the people, many of whom not so long ago were Fitzgo's most enthusiastic backers. "It won't work," he told her. "There must be another way."

He began making telephone calls to his friends to see if any of them wanted a dog. Some lived in apartments and had leases that didn't permit pets. Others already had dogs and didn't want another. Others didn't want any pets.

"And when I told the story about Fitzgo," he said to his wife, "I think some were afraid. They didn't say it like this, but what they were thinking was: 'You want us to adopt a wild dog from Central Park?' They don't know what a fine gentleman he is."

Nine days after the old man had received the certified letter from the management, he kept Fitzgo in the apartment all day. His wife stayed home from work to be with them. They played with the dog; they fed him roast beef that night, roast beef they couldn't eat themselves.

Chapter Eight

THE NEXT MORNING the old man was up early, and Fitzgo was at his side, stretching and yawning. The man warmed a large pan of milk and then heated chunks of roast beef. Fitzgo ate this great breakfast with gusto, wagging his tail.

The old man just looked down at the dog with sorrowful eyes.

He could tell Fitzgo was ready to go outside as the morning hours passed, because of the way he paced back and forth in front of the door. But he couldn't bring himself to take the dog out at the usual time. Finally, about eleven o'clock, the man and the dog went out of the apartment building and into a cold and windy winter day. Steel-gray clouds stood over Central Park, and it didn't take a weatherman to see that before the day was out there would be a storm.

Fitzgo was eager to get into the park, to do his business, to have his daily run. Just as the light turned green the old man reached down and held the dog close to him for just a moment. Fitzgo looked up at the man and then tugged to get away and across the street while the traffic was stopped. "Fitzgo, Fitzgo," the man said softly, his eyes filling with tears. The light turned red. When the light turned back to green he patted the dog on the head and stood up.

The dog must have sensed something was wrong. For a moment he stood still at the man's side. "Go, Fitzgo, go," the man said, softly patting the dog on the rump. The dog slowly crossed the street and when he reached the other side he looked back at the old man.

The old man started to pull his hands from his pockets to wave good-bye to the dog. Instead, he dug his hands deeper into his pockets and headed back for the apartment door.

The gray clouds over Central Park didn't take long to make good on their promise. A half hour later the wind whipped up pieces of paper and hurled them against the vacant park benches and onto the cyclone fences by the baseball diamonds. Then it started: torrents of sleet that rattled on the metal roofs of the park shelters as if someone was throwing buckets of beans from the sky.

Fitzgo was soon back at the apartment door. He bounded up over the two stone steps and stopped suddenly. Looking at him through the double glass doors was the doorman who had almost choked him to death. Fitzgo looked beyond him to see if the old man was wait-

74

ing in the lobby, waiting to take him in as he had done so many times before in bad weather. He paced in front of the door, then finally huddled in the bushes by the steps to shield himself from the sleet that was turning to snow.

A little while later the old man walked past the doorman, who was keeping an eye on Fitzgo, and out onto the steps. Fitzgo leaped out of the bushes, his tail wagging furiously. The old man looked down at him and then turned up the street toward the post office. Fitzgo was at his side, his head turned toward him, waiting for some sign that he knew the dog was there. The man just plunged his hands into his pockets and trudged through the falling snow.

On the way back from the post office the old man found the dog at his side again. As usual. When they reached the front door of the apartment building the doorman was still there, and this time his look moved quickly from the dog to the old man. He stared at the old man to see what he was going to do.

The old man put his foot on the front steps. Then he stopped. He stepped back and dropped to both knees in the slush that had formed on the sidewalk and gave the dog a hug that was so tight Fitzgo let out a wheeze.

Quickly the old man got up and walked into the building, and the doorman slammed the door right behind him. He stopped in the middle of the lobby to look back. What he saw was a dog whose coat was soaked and had flecks of snow on it. A dog with soft brown eyes that were fixed on the door. A dog whose paws were filthy from the mud of the park and the grime of the street. A dog whose once erect tail was now between his legs.

It was the same dog the old man—and many of us in the apartment building—had seen roaming the park just a year before.

A day or two after the old man had been forced to keep Fitzgo out of the building, Joy, on her way back from work, saw the dog standing by the entrance. The coat that the old man had kept so clean was filthy, and chunks of ice hung from the dog's belly where cold rain had frozen. Joy could see that Fitzgo was quaking from the cold. The weather had been miserable the past few days: sleet, rain mixed with snow, and bone-chilling winds.

"I can't figure it out, Paul," she said to me when she got upstairs. "Fitzgo looks like a wreck; maybe the old man's grown tired of him or something. But he's a wreck, all shaking and cold and dirty."

"Probably just stayed out too long in the park," I said as I stuffed some pillows into a box. "The way the old man loves him, you don't have to worry; Fitzgo gets the best of care. Where are those other boxes, the big ones?"

"But he just doesn't look right; something's gone wrong."

"Listen, the dog is fine," I said impatiently. "Let's concentrate on getting the rest of this stuff packed."

"Okay, okay, I got some sandwiches from the deli. Let's eat, pack and try to get out of here before seven."

I had parked the car a few blocks away, so I told Joy to give me a few minutes to come around to the front so we both wouldn't have to go out into the nasty weather. By the time I pulled up in front of our building I could see Joy inside the lobby, talking to an older woman. I expected her to come out when she saw me, but she looked out and held up one finger, to signal she'd just be a minute.

After five minutes of waiting with the motor running I got out of the car and stormed up to the door. I tried to sound patient. "Joy, I think we'd better get moving."

"Okay, okay, Paul," Joy said, "but this lady was wondering the same thing. She never saw Fitzgo looking worse and she's worried. She's going to try to find out what apartment the old man lives in and see if anything's wrong."

"It's funny, I see that man every day and I don't know his name or his apartment," the other woman said.

"We've been out every night lately, working on our house, so we haven't seen him," Joy said.

"Joy, we'd better get—" I started.

"If you find out anything, let me know," Joy said to the other woman. "We're the Wilkeses, and we live in Four-B. If anything is wrong and in case the man doesn't want the dog, we've just bought an old house in Brooklyn and we'd love to have him. So find out if you can, please."

Before we pulled away from the curb, I turned to Joy with a half smile, half frown. "What's this we want the dog business? I mean, I think he's nice and everything, but the old man was the only one who ever had any control over him. We've got a house to fix up, months of work ahead of us; we couldn't take on a dog now."

"I only told her in case, and maybe everything's all right," Joy said, turning on the radio.

Chapter Nine

THE NEXT DAY I came up out of the subway after work and made my way as fast as I could to the apartment building. It was another snowy, slushy day in New York; everything was gray and dripping or frosted. The bushes along the street next to Central Park drooped under the weight of the heavy snow. The sidewalks were gray, soupy puddles of half-melted snow.

Joy and I had a lot of work to do that night. The final clean-up on the row house in Brooklyn had to be finished. We had been working on it for over a month, and it was still a mess. It would take us many months to get it into shape but we were excited about it. After living in apartments for the first six years of our married life, this would be our own house.

My mind was on the stacks of boxes that sat in our apartment on the fourth floor and on the chunks of plaster and pieces of wood that were still in our brownstone and had to be thrown out before tomorrow. My mind was on the movers who were coming the first thing next morning. They cost $35 an hour and we wanted the move to go as quickly and as cheaply as possible.

So, as the elevator doors opened on my floor and I made a right turn toward our apartment, my mind was swimming with the many things that were going to occur in the next twenty-four hours.

And there he was.

There was Fitzgo, pacing frantically—almost running up and down the hall—with a wild and confused look in his eyes. His tail was between his legs and his fur was streaked with murky grays and browns. Fitzgo looked as if he had just been dragged through the park. My first feeling was fear. He looked as if he'd attack anybody who touched him.

I stayed close to the wall, and when I got to the apartment I rang the bell and yelled, "He's . . . he's out here, Joy!"

"Who's out . . . ?" Joy started to say as she came running and opened the door. Her question was answered as she saw the dog down the hall, still pacing frantically.

"Stay away from him," I said. "He really looks wild tonight."

"He's never hurt anybody, Paul; something's wrong, just as I thought."

"Look at those eyes; something is wrong, but let's stay out of this."

"Where did you find him?"

"Just came up to the floor and there he was."

"We've got to hold onto him and find the old man and see what gives."

"Joy, look at that dog; he's wild-eyed. He could have rabies or anything."

"Come, Fitzgo, come, good dog; it's okay," Joy said softly, holding out her hand.

Fitzgo looked and came toward her. Then he turned away and started pacing again.

"Maybe the old man is sick or something, Paul. Let's just find out and then we can get out to the house. We can't leave the dog walking around on the floor. Somebody will call the doorman and this time he'll choke Fitzgo to death."

"I don't know, Joy, he looks wrong to me."

"Just help me get him inside. Help me find the old man and then we'll go. Please, Paul. Please. I couldn't sleep tonight wondering if he's all right or not."

"Well, okay," I said hesitantly, "but let's get going. We've got at least five hours of work ahead of us. And don't get so close to him. The dog can bite you, Joy. Let's just be a little careful. Promise?"

"Promise. Promise." Joy was already inside the apartment, taking some of the corned beef out of her sandwich. "Here, Fitzgo, come here, Fitz," she called to the dog.

She moved down the hallway toward the dog, who had kept up his pacing. He slowed down as she came close to him. She held out the meat and he sniffed it, then moved away.

"Careful, Joy," I called from the door of our apartment.

"Fitz, it's okay," Joy said, reaching out with her hand, palm up. The dog came to her and sniffed the hand and once again moved away. Joy went to the dog and sat on the floor near him. She reached out and touched him softly on the head, and this time he didn't retreat.

Joy extended a piece of the corned beef, and Fitzgo sniffed it first, then took it from her fingers. "There's more, Fitz; come on in. There's lots more." She kept her hand out with a piece of corned beef in it and started to back up toward our apartment. Fitzgo followed by a few feet.

Joy stepped inside the apartment and gave a piece of the meat to the dog, which was still standing in the hallway. "Come on now, Fitz, and we'll have some more." The dog stood outside the door and looked warily inside. Every few seconds he shot a look down the hallway.

Fitzgo wouldn't budge. So Joy just reached out, patted him on the head and then, with a firm hold on the back of his head, pulled him into the apartment and closed the door.

"Joy!" I gasped when I saw her grabbing the dog, but before I could say anything else, Fitzgo was in the apartment and the door was closed.

"He could have bitten your arm off," I said.

"He's not that way; he's just scared. Now let's put the rest of that corned beef into a bowl; he looks hungry. Then we've got to find the old man."

Joy put the bowl on the floor, but after taking a few bites Fitzgo wasn't interested in food any more. He began to pace back and forth in the small kitchen. Joy stayed with the dog, and I volunteered to go to the lobby, hoping to find someone who might know the old man's name or his apartment.

When I got to the lobby no one was there except one of the janitors, who was mopping the floor.

"You know the old man who sometimes comes in here with that white-and-brown dog?" I asked.

"Youa mean da Fitzgo," the man replied in English that was tinged with his native Italian.

"Yes, yes," I said. "What's his name?"

"Name?" the janitor said, a puzzled look on his face. "I no knowa his name. Some funny name. Slovak, no?"

"I think so. Where does he live? Do you know what apartment he lives in?"

"Where?" And the same puzzled look came over his face. "I no knowa where. But . . ."

I waited for him to find the right words.

"I moppa da ninth floor today and da old man, he get offa da elevator. But I no knowa what apartment he go to."

"That's a start. Thanks a lot," I said as I started back toward the elevator.

When I got back to our apartment, Fitzgo still hadn't slowed down.

"He hasn't touched the food, either," Joy said. "Did you have any luck?"

"The janitor downstairs says the old man lives on the ninth floor. Do you suppose Fitzgo . . . ?"

Joy read my thoughts. "Let's give it a try."

She coaxed Fitzgo onto the elevator, and luckily there were no other calls for it, so we went straight to the ninth floor. As soon as the door opened the dog shot

83 🎋

out and, slipping and sliding on the clean tile, turned to the right and stopped suddenly in front of 9C.

Joy and I looked at each other. "It's going to be mighty hard to explain this if we don't have the right apartment," I said.

Joy shrugged. "No choice, I guess."

I rang the buzzer.

In a few seconds, we could hear someone inside. Then the door slowly opened.

Fitzgo's tail, which had been between his legs, rose up and started wagging furiously even before we could see who was opening the door.

As soon as the crack was wide enough for a dog to get through, Fitzgo was inside the apartment. "Fitzgo, my Fitzgo," came the voice from inside.

With the door opened wider, we could see the old man standing inside.

We hardly knew what to say. "We . . . well, the dog was on our floor today and he . . . well . . . he looked so muddy and everything . . . we didn't know . . ." Joy stammered.

"Come in," he said simply. "I will tell you why."

The old man and his wife sat on an overstuffed sofa, and Fitzgo soon curled up at their feet and went to sleep. Then the old man told the whole sad story: the doorman, the ten-day eviction notice, his attempts to find Fitzgo a home.

"On the tenth day I took him out and I felt worse than ever before in my life. I came back and he wanted to come in and I had to turn my back on him. I called the animal shelter and they said they would come for the dog, but if nobody adopted him in ten days they would have to put him to sleep."

His voice started to crack.

"He was able to survive a year in the park; maybe he can do it again. I didn't like it when people called him wild, but maybe there is enough wild blood in him to survive. I will feed him every day, but I can't bring him in."

"Or else all of us will be living in Central Park," his wife said. Although she was half trying to make a joke, none of us could even smile.

"This is a very special dog," the old man said. "I have prayed for him. Somehow he will survive. Somehow. . . ."

Joy looked at me, and it was one of those times when words weren't needed.

"Sir," Joy started, "we know Fitzgo is very attached to you. After all, you were the one who tamed him. And you are the only one who can really feed him. But, you see, we've bought a house in Brooklyn and we're moving tomorrow. If you think Fitzgo would come we would love to have him live with us."

Tears filled the old man's eyes. "I don't care about the eviction. The dog spends this night with me," he said. "I will give him a fine bath, and tomorrow he will be ready for his new home."

Then he looked down at the dog sleeping at his feet.

"See, Fitzgo, I told you our prayers would be answered."

Chapter Ten

I HADN'T really thought about having a pet in our new home, but in those few minutes it had all been worked out. Fitzgo needed a home. Joy had loved the dog from the first time she saw him in the park. And he was beginning to look like less of a wolf to me. More like a good old tramp mutt. Yes, Joy had been convincing me—and so had Fitzgo—that he was a dog with strange but likable characteristics. We knew the old man would miss Fitzgo, so we promised he could visit him any time he wanted to.

But Fitzgo?

How would he adjust to his new home? Would a dog who had let only one person feed him allow us to take care of him? Would he want to run away from us and somehow find his way back to the old man or to Central Park, where he had lived most of his life? Would he make a trip like *The Incredible Journey* to get back to the old man? Would he feel penned in? Although we had Prospect Park nearby we couldn't let him run free there. First, he didn't know the park and second, neither of us was home during the day to let him back in.

The next evening, with the back seat of our car loaded with the plants that the movers couldn't take plus little odds and ends, we were ready for our trip to Brooklyn with Fitzgo—and all those questions unanswered.

Sure enough, when the old man opened the door, we could see that the dog had been bathed; his white coat seemed whiter that night than we had ever seen it before.

"I thought Fitzgo might be nervous for the trip," the old man said, "so I gave him half of a sleeping pill in his food tonight. Look at his eyes, he is already drowsy.

"Come, I will take him down to the car for you and get him settled down. Please bring his water and food bowls," he said to his wife. "Also, the collar. He no longer fights the collar. He will wear it for you, I am sure. But let's not put it on him this last time."

Joy and I got into the car, and the old man picked Fitzgo up and wiped off his paws with his handkerchief. The dog looked at him through his half-closed eyes and lazily lapped his friend across the cheek with his tongue. Then the old man moved toward the open door and tried to put the dog on Joy's lap. Fitzgo stiffened. His legs shot out straight. His eyes opened wide.

"Good dog, my Fitzgo, these people will take care of you," he said in a calm voice. He patted the dog on the head and again tried to put him in the car. Again the dog stiffened, but the old man went ahead and put the dog on Joy's lap.

Fitzgo was shaking so badly he rattled the buttons on Joy's coat. When the old man reached in to touch the dog for the last time, Fitzgo tried to jump back into his arms.

"No, Fitzgo, you must go. You must go now." He shut the door, and as we pulled away Joy looked back to see the old man and his wife waving until we turned the corner.

The trip to Brooklyn was, to say the least, unforgettable.

The sleeping pill made Fitzgo yawn often, and between the shaking and the yawning and the huffing and his high whines, we really wondered if he would make the trip in one piece. When we started across the Brooklyn Bridge our tires hit the bridge's steel plating, which caused a high-pitched squeal. Fitzgo, his eyes bulging, jumped off Joy's lap and onto the floor, and there he cowered for the last fifteen minutes of our trip. At least the windshield got a chance to clear; his huffing was now directed toward the floor.

When we reached the house and Joy had scooped Fitzgo up off the floor, we wondered what his first reaction would be in a new place. We set him down inside, and after about ten minutes the shaking stopped. A half hour later the whimpering stopped . . . at least for a while.

He cautiously nosed around the gaping holes in the plaster and sniffed at the eighty or ninety years of smells stored in them. It really wasn't much of a home—even for a vagabond dog. We were willing to put up with it while we remodeled, but we wondered if the noise and clutter and, most of all, confinement wouldn't send Fitzgo looking for a way out.

Fitzgo paid no attention to us as we carried the plants into the house and arranged the boxes the movers had brought in that morning.

"I wonder what's going through his brain," Joy said, looking at Fitzgo, who had stopped wandering around the house and had settled down on some dirty cleaning rags under a table.

"Utter, total, complete confusion," I said, "tied together with a good dose of fear. Look at him huffing, and it's not even sixty degrees in here. By the way, the furnace again?"

"Guess so. We must have hit the thermostat when we were moving the stuff," Joy replied. We had torn down the wall that the thermostat was mounted on, so it hung crazily from the ceiling in the middle of the room. We were constantly hitting it and causing the furnace to turn off.

"Maybe he's found a home," I said, looking at him under the table.

"Hate to see him on those filthy rags."

"Our work clothes are dirtier than those rags. Fitz is just going to have to live like we do for the next few months."

We worked on the first floor until about midnight that night, and when we were ready to go to where our bed was—we couldn't call it a bedroom; it was just a clear spot where we could fit the frame and mattress—we slowly went up the stairs, shuffling our feet. We wanted Fitzgo to know we were going to the second floor. By the time we were halfway up the stairs he was at the bottom, still huffing.

"Come on, Fitz, time for bed; let's go," Joy called to him. He didn't move. He just stared at us with a look that appeared to be both afraid and puzzled. And he was whining steadily again, as he had done in the car.

"Let's go up, Joy," I said. "If he wants to come, he can. Maybe he wants to be alone tonight."

"Do you think he might do anything downstairs?" Joy said, and then a grin crossed her face. "He couldn't do anything worse than we've already done with sledge hammers and crowbars."

We got ready for bed—which mainly consisted of hanging our work clothes over a chair and shaking off the excess plaster from our bedspread—and Joy decided to give Fitzgo one last call.

There he was, still whining, still standing at the bottom of the stairs. Joy called to him. She went halfway down and called again. She went almost to the bottom and said softly, "Come on, Fitz, we have to get to sleep and we don't need that lullaby." He seemed to want to come with Joy, but something was holding him back.

"We have to let him get comfortable, Joy, feel his own way. But I could do without his whining. If he could just talk and tell us what he wants, I'd be happy to supply it to get a good night's sleep."

There was no shutting doors to keep the sound away

from us; at that point, all the doors but one had been removed.

"He's not happy, that's for sure, Paul."

"Maybe he's not happy with our service, Joy. Maybe he expects to be carried upstairs for bed."

"That's it!" Joy said.

"What's it?"

Joy picked up Fitzgo and carried him up the stairs to the second floor.

"Now wait a minute; let's not start spoiling him the first night," I said indignantly.

"Remember how he used to jump over the two steps from the street to the lobby at the apartment?" Joy asked.

"Never noticed."

"This dog doesn't know how to climb stairs. The car ride, too. The reason he was so frightened is that he's never been in a car before. Paul, we have the original culturally deprived city dog."

That night wasn't the most restful for either of us. Fitzgo stalked around the second floor, and we kept waking up to the crunch of plaster under his paws. There were no curtains on the window, so the sun woke us the next morning. And there, his head resting on the edge of the bed on Joy's side, was Fitzgo. He was motionless, just watching us as we slowly woke up.

He had been a gentleman during the night and hadn't dirtied our dirty house any more than it already was. As we came downstairs we thought he would follow us, but we had forgotten. There he stood at the top of the stairs, a low whine in his nostrils.

"Better bring down Mr. Culturally Deprived," I said to Joy. "Steps have been around for centuries; hope this dog catches on soon."

I knew that the old man had fed the dog well—roast beef, chicken parts, tasty Czech dishes—but one thing was firm in my mind. In our house Fitzgo would be a dog and he would eat dog food. Cheap dog food, at that.

"After all, Joy, he ate scraps in the park and he did okay," I said, frying some eggs for us. "I'm not buying that all-meat kind of dog food at forty-five cents a can. He gets the fifteen-cent kind and he'll like it. Now don't be surprised if he doesn't go for it this morning, but we can't give in. He'll get hungry and he'll eat it sooner or later. Don't be worried."

I had rehearsed that talk on the economics of dog food. The television commercials about the expensive "all meat" brands always got me angry. Dogs would eat what you put before them, was my thought on the subject. Human beings spoiled their pets into wanting special kinds of foods, and I wasn't going to fall for it. Throughout my speech Joy was quiet.

I opened the can of dog food and emptied it into his dish. "He'll get used to it. He might not eat it right away, but he'll get used to it. Don't worry."

Joy remained silent.

I put the bowl down. Fitzgo walked over to it, sniffed the dog food once and began eating. He finished it and had the bowl licked clean in less than a minute.

Joy smiled at me. "Culturally deprived dog's a bargain, right, Paul?"

Chapter Eleven

F ITZGO'S FIRST DAY in our home was a Friday; Joy had the day off from school, but I had to go to work. The plumbers and electricians were going to be in the house that day, so we were happy that one of us could stay home with Fitzgo. It would be a noisy day filled with strange people and a lot of coming and going—which worried us most. An open door might be Fitzgo's invitation to leave his new and rather mixed-up home.

After we finished breakfast, Joy put the collar around his neck and we decided we would both take him for the morning walk. We wanted to be prepared for anything, and two of us could handle Fitz better if he tried to run away.

We opened the door and then the iron gate in the small entryway. Fitzgo sniffed the air. A half inch of snow had fallen the night before; Fitzgo cautiously stepped out and slowly walked toward the sidewalk. His tail—the easiest way to tell how he felt at any particular moment—wasn't high in the air, wasn't between his legs; it was at an uncertain half mast.

"What does the book say about this one?" Joy asked. "How do you train a pure-bred city dog who had the run of the park to learn the rules of the street?"

Fitz sniffed at some bushes in front of the house—those were off limits—so Joy eased him over toward the curb and I kept between him and the houses as we walked down the street. He walked slowly and then picked up, catching another scent. Before we knew it, he was in the curb, between the parked cars, his nose to the ground.

Joy and I grinned at one another. It couldn't be this easy, could it?

For the next ten minutes, Fitzgo dodged in and out between the parked cars. He had the right idea—that was the place to go—but he just didn't seem ready to make the commitment.

"Hate to have to take him up to the park every day," I said to Joy.

She agreed. "Those three blocks would be awfully long on rainy mornings. No, he's got to go in the street like all the other dogs."

We kept on walking; Fitzgo kept on sniffing. Finally —and I'll never forget the two cars; one was a green Volkswagen and the other was a light blue Ford—Fitzgo did what he was there to do. That may not seem like the most important thing in the world, but training a dog to curb in the city sometimes takes months and we were facing the coldest months of the year. For some reason, instinct told Fitzgo where he must go.

As we got back near our house, Fitzgo put a strain on the leash. Although all the houses on our block look pretty much alike, he turned at the entrance to ours even before we started in.

When Joy took off his collar inside the house, he shook violently as if to shake off the cold and went back to see if there were any last bits of his breakfast in his bowl. A few laps of water followed and he walked back to the table and bedded down on the dirty rags.

It was already nine o'clock, time for me to be at work. My boss wasn't very strict about my being on time, but that morning I stopped in his office to tell him why I was late. We both had a good laugh about it.

I called Joy about noon to see how Fitz had done that far.

"I just sat with him and stroked him and used the brush the old man had, and he seemed to relax," Joy said. "I talked to him. What did I say? Oh, I don't know, just 'You're a good dog and you'll like it here and we'll take good care of you.' That kind of stuff. He seemed pretty calm. Then the electricians came in with their boxes of equipment and spools of wire and those pipes they put the wires into, and Fitzgo really started barking. Hair up on the back of his neck and everything.

"They said I should lock him up while they worked. I told them he always did that when he saw big tools and stuff; I was talking like we had the dog for ten years.

I told them he'd calm down in a few minutes. And he did. I just stayed with him and kept on stroking him and talking to him. He was a little wild-eyed when they started bashing holes in the ceiling to locate the old lines so I kept him up on the second floor till now."

When I got home near six o'clock, Joy filled me in on the rest of the day. "The plumbers came in the afternoon, and they brought in a huge piece of equipment for threading their pipes. His whole back was up; he barked and barked," Joy said. "He was at the top of the stairs and I wondered, if he knew how to get down the stairs, whether he would have done anything."

"It's funny he's like that," I said. "He never barked at people in the park."

"It must have something to do with having four walls around him and no place to go. Or maybe he's protective. Who knows?"

That Saturday and Sunday, Joy and I worked from nine in the morning until nearly midnight. We tore up old flooring that was rotten from years of moisture. We chipped away at the old tile and plaster to get to the brick beneath, which would give the house a rustic look. We started to strip the layers of paint off the shutters and doors to bring back the original oak and mahogany that had been hidden for many decades.

Through all the work, Fitzgo usually stayed at Joy's side; when she was working near the table, he would bed down beneath it. The pattern was forming: Fitzgo was going to be closer to Joy. She was the one who had tried to make friends with him in the park; she had eventually petted him; she had held him on the first trip to Brooklyn; she had spent the first day getting him settled in this new, strange house.

Monday presented another problem. We both would be at our jobs, and another workman would be in the house. He was to put in a new ceiling that was made in one of the original tin patterns the house had when it was built in 1880. We didn't know what Fitzgo would do with a stranger in the house and neither of us there.

The one door that was still on its hinges on the second floor blocked off one exit and where another door had once been in place we piled cardboard boxes and leaned the door against them. It would give Fitzgo a big area to roam and yet keep him contained.

We told the workman about the dog and not to worry about him, that he might make some noise but he would stay on the second floor during the day. Smitty was the man's name, and as he wrapped a big blue handkerchief over his hair to keep his head clean during his dusty job, he said, "Don't bother me none. I like dogs."

Joy and I both got home about five thirty that night and Smitty was just washing up. Half the ceiling was already in place, and we were admiring his work when we heard a familiar whine. There was Fitzgo at the top of the stairs, looking down on us.

"He howled all morning, then he would whine, and I heard a lot of shuffling up there," Smitty said. "When I sat down to eat my lunch on the stairs, there he was, just like he is now."

"He either opened a door or moved a pile of cardboard boxes," I said, letting Smitty out.

We went upstairs.

"Don't show him any affection yet, Joy; let's see what he's done and then . . . and then we'll decide whether to punish him or what."

The one door on the floor was still closed. We went down the hall and stepped through a hole in the wall where double doors had once been and looked at the only other place he could have come through. The door that had held the cardboard boxes in place had been pushed to one side. The pile of boxes that had been neatly stacked were a jumbled heap. At the side of two of the boxes, we could see scraps of cardboard and scraps of blankets.

Joy and I looked at each other in dismay. Joy turned to Fitzgo, who was right behind her, and said in a low, sure voice, "That was a bad, bad dog. *Bad.*" She pointed to the shreds of cardboard. "Did you do this?" I looked at the hunks of blanket and then I looked around on the floor for something to hit the dog with. I felt my forehead and cheeks getting hot. An old *Life* magazine was in the corner and I rolled it up, ready to let Fitzgo know that he wasn't going to demolish things whenever he wasn't happy with being locked up.

I turned to go after him. And there he was, already on his back, his paws up in the air, his head turned aside, his tail curled so tightly between his legs it looked as if it were glued to him.

I raised my hand.

He let out a whimper and just lay there.

I raised my hand again.

Another whimper.

"It's no use, Joy," I said, lowering my hand. "I can't hit him. He knows he did wrong. What's the use of beating him?"

"Captivity," Joy said, looking inside the box to see how badly the blankets had been damaged. "He'll do anything to get free when he thinks he's being held in captivity. Look, Paul, he only really worked over that cheap pink blanket we never use and took a little hunk out of the blue one. It's not the end of the world."

"Guess not," I said. "He'll have to run free and we'll just have to let the workmen know that he'll be up here."

In New York City you treat skilled craftsmen with great care because: (1) good ones are hard to find; (2) they are very expensive, and (3) they can make your renovation move along easily or make it a nightmare, depending on how they feel about you. So we were very careful in telling the men who worked in our house that Fitzgo might bark a bit but he wouldn't harm them and he would stay up on the second floor anyway.

That seemed to work out well. Fitzgo did get used to the workmen being on the first floor but he also had learned how to climb the stairs. That happened the middle of the first week he was there. One night as we were going up to bed, Joy called to him. He looked at the stairs, drew back and made a leap toward them as if he wanted to take all thirteen steps in one bound. It took four or five bounds that first time, but gradually he learned that one or two at a time was easier.

After we were in the house two weeks, Joy's father came from California to help us with some of the work. When he walked in and saw the gaping holes in the walls and wires hanging from the ceiling, he wondered if we knew what we were doing. Quite honestly, much of the time we didn't, but we learned as we went along.

Joy's father had spent his first forty years as a Nebraska farmer, and he loved animals and took to Fitzgo right away. "Come here, fella," he said to Fitzgo. Joy's father took the dog's head in both his hands and rubbed his thumbs along the white streak on top. Fitzgo half closed his eyes in pleasure. "Remember Brownie on the farm, Joy? He used to like that. Good boy, Fitzgo; you and I are going to get along just fine."

And they did. Fitzgo followed Joy's father around the house during the day as he did his work—until about four o'clock. Then Fitzgo would go to the top of the stairs on the second floor and lie down; from there he could see the front door. And when it opened and Joy came in—she was usually home first—he would scramble down the stairs, yipping and wagging his tail. His way of greeting her was to rise up on his back legs and wiggle in the air. As he was a gentleman, he never jumped up on her; just those wiggles and yips of delight. Joy would put her books down and stroke Fitzgo a bit, and soon he would be calm.

Chapter Twelve

As we began to meet our neighbors on our walks with Fitzgo we told them his history, and often they were more interested in hearing about this wild dog of Central Park than they were in learning about us, the new people on the street. Fitzgo was better known on the block than we were, and people who didn't know our names would often say, "Oh, yes, you're the couple with Fitzgo, the Central Park dog. What's your name again?"

Fitzgo proved to be a good neighbor. His curb habits were made to order, and as the months progressed he was ready, even eager, to be petted by anyone. Little children would pull his ears or his tail, and Fitzgo would just gently nuzzle them in return.

"If a year ago somebody had told me that the wild dog I was watching would someday be living with us and would be the kind of dog he is, I would have laughed at them," Joy said one night during dinner. "He's the perfect dog."

"Almost," I replied. "When we get the house finished and we can start reading something else besides handyman's books, I want to see if he'll curl up at our feet. Then I'll say he's perfect."

"A couple more months and you'll have the chance to find out."

The renovation was going well as the cold months passed and we moved into spring. Walls were being closed up, wood was showing after many hours of paint removing, light fixtures were being attached to wires in the ceiling, the tile was in place in the bathroom.

We lived through those months of dirt and dust with good humor—most of the time—and so did Fitz. He developed a couple of habits I wasn't too happy with, but Joy had a way of explaining them to me. For instance, he always barked when the doorbell rang. And Fitzgo had an ear-piercing bark. "He's just welcoming people we know or scaring away somebody who might be checking to see if nobody is home so they could rob us."

He barked every morning when the mailman stuffed mail into our box and three mornings a week when the garbage man picked up the cans. "Protecting us; he is just protecting us," Joy would say.

In spring our back yard, which was then little more than a patch of high grass and weeds, sprouted a few flowers. And the wild rosebushes along the fence blossomed early that year. When we'd be working in the back yard, we'd often see Fitzgo sniffing the flowers. He really loved flowers.

Besides being a good companion in the back yard who could give us some pleasant moments by just watching him, he also kept the cats out. We really have nothing against cats, but a neighbor told us that once they take a liking to your patch of weeds, and do their business there every day, the smell isn't to be believed. So Fitz sent his share of cats up and over the fence.

We learned a lot about Fitzgo in those six months while we were renovating the house. For one thing, he would not allow us to teach him any tricks. Almost every dog you know can roll over, or jump through a hoop, or sit up or bark on command. Not Fitz. We tried for hours to get him to chase a rubber ball. He would just watch it roll by and then look at us. Right in the eyes. It was either a case of "You can't teach an old dog new tricks" or he was just too much of a gentleman, too dignified in his own way, to be a part of such foolishness. He would always come when we called him, but that was about the extent of his "training."

He was not hard to live with; he made few demands. For sure, he wasn't temperamental. Except for one time. At the end of one work day, when we were just too exhausted to do anything after dinner, Joy pulled her violin out of its dusty case and ran a few scales before beginning a soothing classical piece. At the first sounds of the violin, Fitzgo perked up his ears, then gave a low whine as if his ears were being hurt. He disappeared upstairs and Joy continued to play, figuring that if he wanted some distance from the sound he could have it. Minutes later he came down the stairs, a pillow from our bed in his mouth. He stared at Joy, then dropped the pillow at her feet, backed away, settled down on his haunches, but continued to stare at her. Once we realized what had happened, Joy and I both laughed about it and said that Fitzgo could have been a little more kind in showing his displeasure for either that particular musical instrument or Joy's playing.

It didn't take long for us to realize that Fitzgo really wasn't the free roamer that we believed he would always be. He wasn't a wild dog at all. When we'd let him off the leash on our way back to the house, he would always beat us there. He never tried to run away. He liked the security, the warmth of a home. He liked regular meals.

But anything that came close to real captivity, he fought. One day I was walking Fitzgo and I wanted to get something in the grocery store, so I hooked his chain onto a parking meter in front of the store. As I went in he tried to follow me, but the chain became taut and jerked him back. He suddenly had that wild look in his eyes that I remembered from so many months before. I went back to him and patted him on the head. "It's all right, Fitz; I'm going right in there. I'll be out in two minutes."

I came out of the store and the chain and collar were there, but Fitz was gone.

When I got back to the house there was Fitz at the front door, his tail between his legs, looking at me sheepishly. He had somehow gotten out of the collar. When that meter was holding him captive, something inside him clicked and he had to escape.

Wherever our bed was during those months—and it moved from place to place—Fitzgo would always sleep beside it, always on Joy's side. And each morning, his head would be resting on the edge of the bed, his eyes watching us; Fitzgo would be waiting for us to get up. If we slept late he never once tried to wake us. If we got up early, he would always be ready to go.

He had a funny sleeping habit. We had a dropcloth over the table next to the bed, and Fitz would scoot underneath and sleep so that his head and shoulders were covered. We wondered if that came from his time in Central Park when he could only keep part of his body dry or if it gave him the feeling that he was in a lair and somehow protected from the outside world. Whatever caused him to do it, he slept that way every night.

Joy is one of those people who doesn't exactly bounce out of bed in the morning. Waking up is a painful and slow process for her. So, as part of her waking-up routine each morning, she would pet Fitzgo on the head; then she would scratch him on the back, at the base of the tail, where he liked it so much. And Fitzgo would show his pleasure by skimming his face along the papers or rags or whatever was alongside the bed. He really seemed to be in paradise about it. And, because Joy had to reach out from beneath the warm blankets, it cut at least five minutes from her normal "waking up" time.

When Fitzgo would fall asleep before we did, he would do strange things some nights. His nose would begin to twitch; then his jowls would start flapping as he exhaled heavily. Then his body would contort and tense up and he would yip softly. He seemed to be having a dog's nightmare, somehow recalling experiences in the park that we probably didn't even know about. It made us sad to see him like that, and we would always wake him, pet him and let him fall back to sleep again, hoping he would not have another nightmare.

Needless to say, Fitzgo was very much a part of our life. He was living through rough days with us. He was always good-natured, excited to see us when we came home from our jobs. When something in the house wasn't going right, Joy or I could sit down with Fitz and just by petting him and having him lean up against us we could get a good feeling from him and find the strength to go back to the job that seemed impossible.

During the early months of the renovation the old man called many times, asking how the dog was doing, if he was eating, if we were giving him chicken livers and hearts, if Fitzgo was talking to us.

We had to be honest with him. Yes, the dog was getting along fine, but no, he wasn't on any special diet and, if he was doing any talking, we weren't very good listeners because we hadn't heard anything.

He often would ask us if we could bring Fitzgo in to see him, as it was difficult for him to come to Brooklyn. "Some evening, perhaps when you want to go to a movie or something, leave the dog here for a few hours," he offered more than once.

There wasn't time for movies and such treats during

the early stages, but finally about halfway through we decided to go out on a Friday night. I called the old man and he was very happy. "I will go get the chicken livers and hearts right now and have them ready for him. And another thing; my wife and I have been thinking. We might buy a house and then we can keep Fitzgo with us again."

"Oh," was all I could say.

Joy knew that something was wrong at the sound of that word.

"What is it?" She looked at me.

"Impossible. After all this time. He couldn't."

"What, Paul, what is it?"

"The old man is talking about buying a house. And then taking Fitzgo back to live with him."

Joy looked down at Fitzgo, who was dozing close to the wall where the air vent from the furnace kept a spot warm. "No, no. He wouldn't. He couldn't."

Three days later we were driving across the Brooklyn Bridge, the only sounds being the car's engine, the tires on the grating and Fitzgo's huffing in the back seat. He never did learn to relax in a car and would huff nervously from the time he got in—and he got in readily—until he got out.

As we approached our old apartment building, I said, "Well, how should we handle this?"

"We just can't walk in there and say, 'We'll be back in three hours and don't you have any funny ideas about keeping this dog,'" Joy said. "I don't want to hurt the old man's feelings. But we have to do something that makes it clear he's our dog now."

"How to do that is the problem," I said, immediately feeling how stupid my words were.

We parked near the apartment entrance, and Fitzgo jumped out of the car and headed for the door. He hadn't forgotten. We walked through the lobby and a few people remembered him.

"I always wondered what happened to that dog; thought he got killed or something," one young woman said. "He looks better than ever."

"Brooklyn, huh?" joked an old man. "Thought that dog would never leave Central Park. But he's made the adjustment, huh?"

I assured him he had adjusted fine as I pushed the elevator button, wondering whether a readjustment, back to his first friend, was going to have to happen.

When the elevator opened on the ninth floor, Fitzgo walked quickly out, turned right and soon was standing in front of the old man's door, his tail wagging slightly.

For once seeing Fitzgo happy made us sad.

We rang the bell. The old man must have been waiting right inside. He threw the door open. "Fitzgo, my Fitzgo, my Fitzgo; you have come to see me." Fitzgo ran to him and lapped at his hands.

We stood in the doorway and said nothing.

"Come in." The old man motioned to us. "Fitzgo, you look skinny; I don't think you eat enough. We'll take care of that tonight. All the chicken livers and hearts you can eat."

"We took him to a veterinarian for a check-up and

he said thirty pounds is a good weight, and that's what he weighs now," I said weakly.

"Still he looks skinny. But otherwise good. You have been very good to my dog. He looks just about as good as when I lent him to you in January."

At the word "lent," Joy and I looked at each other. Neither of us could say a thing.

"We have called some real estate men in New Jersey, and in a couple of weeks we are going to see some houses. We hope to find one that we can afford. And then Fitzgo can have a big back yard to run around in and he won't have to breathe the dirty city air any more. It will be good for him, don't you think?"

"Yes, that would be nice, sir," Joy began, "but, you see, we've grown very attached to the dog. He has really been fun to have around. We would miss him very much."

"I know," the old man said, "just as I have missed him all these months. I know the feeling well. But you have a car; you can visit him as often as you like."

We left the building in silence, then mumbled a few words on the way to a movie I don't even remember seeing. When we got back to the front of the building, I said, "It's not going to be like this, Joy. He's our dog. The man didn't lend him, he gave him gladly, so that Fitz wouldn't die out in the park. We're not just going to turn him back over now."

"You don't have to convince me, Paul, but what do we say? That man has so little in his life. Fitzgo was a real friend to him."

The ride to the ninth floor seemed too quick this

time. When we got to the old man's door we hesitated, as if to give each other a last moment for some great thought to dawn that would solve the problem. As we stood there, we could hear a faint whimpering inside.

I rang the bell and Fitz barked loudly. The old man opened the door and Fitzgo squeezed through the small opening and did his leaping, squirming dance on the slippery tile in front of Joy. The old man stood inside the door, no trace of a smile on his face.

"You had a good time, sir, with Fitz?" Joy said.

"Yes, it was good to see him," the old man said, "but . . ."

"But what?" Joy asked.

"He has changed. Once you left, he started crying and he has not stopped till now. I made him chicken livers and hearts and he won't even smell them. I tried to hold him to pet him and all he could do was go to the door and cry for you to come back. I know what he is saying with a cry like that. I can understand him."

"He always whimpers a little bit when we leave him in the house," Joy said.

"But with me?" the old man said, his voice lower. "I was the one who saved him, the one who first fed him. With me, I would never expect such a thing."

"He has been with us for quite a while," I said.

"Yes, and it shows," the old man said. "He loves you; he is happy with you. I guess he is . . . he is . . . your dog now. It was just a dream to think he could come back to me. It is he who chooses who he wants to live with. And he has chosen you."

"But you will see more of him once our work is finished on the house," I said. "These months have been busy. We'll bring him again."

"And I will enjoy each visit," the old man said, "but it will only be a visit. He is your dog now."

The old man put on his coat and we all went down to the car. I opened up the back and Fitzgo jumped right in and started huffing.

"I remember his last trip from here in this car," the old man said. "Yes, he is yours now, and you are very lucky to have such a fine dog. Bring him to see me soon." With that the old man walked back toward the apartment building.

Fitzgo watched him through the rear window, but once I started the car the dog turned and faced forward —away from Central Park and toward Brooklyn.

Chapter Thirteen

To MANY PEOPLE painting and wallpapering are drudgery. To Joy and me, these jobs were joyful events. They showed us the renovation of our row house was in its final stages. Even after working ten or twelve hours at other jobs, we could always find enough energy to paint a wall or a ceiling. We called it "dessert," and we were opening paint cans when our neighbors were getting ready for bed.

I can still remember the day in July when the big event occurred: the red carpeting was laid in the front hallway. That meant our dirty work was over. Floors were refinished; furniture was uncovered; shutters were in place; the gooey job of paint removal was done.

The carpet installers arrived early in the morning and worked until midafternoon. Where rough, stained wood faced us in the morning, a smooth, rich red covering was there at night. It was almost miraculous. It seemed to transform the whole house. It was the one thing that was needed to tell us in no uncertain terms that we were finished with the major work.

After the workmen left Joy and I took off our shoes and walked on the new rug, walked up and down the stairs, which were now padded and no longer squeaked under our weight. We were like children running our toes through the sand at the beach.

"I don't know if I'll ever be able to wear shoes when I walk on it," Joy said.

"It seems too good for just walking on, doesn't it?" I replied.

"Give us a couple weeks; then maybe—maybe—we'll walk on it with shoes."

We fixed our supper that night and forgot about getting Fitzgo's. He would never beg at the table, but if he hadn't been fed by the time we ate he would lie in a certain place by the sink where he could keep his eyes on us. He would cross his paws and put his head on them and just look at us. It was his gentle hint not to forget that he hadn't been fed.

While we were cleaning up the dishes, I remembered and opened a can of dog food for Fitzgo and put it in his bowl in the laundry room. As usual he was right behind me as I took the food in, and he went right at it.

Joy and I were admiring the new rug when Fitzgo walked between us, headed for the front door. A few steps in front of us, he suddenly put the side of his mouth to the new carpeting and skidded along. Then the other side of his mouth, and he started to skid again.

"Fitz!" I yelled. He stopped short. His tail went

between his legs and he slunk into the living room and lay down, looking at us sheepishly out of the corner of his eye.

"That dog," Joy said, a smile coming across her face.

"I don't think it's that funny; his greasy old mouth on that new rug," I said. "That's got to stop."

"He's got more sense than we do, Paul."

"Sense? That makes sense?"

"He's been waiting six months for a place to wipe his mouth. Remember in the park how he used to skid along the grass after a meal? He's just telling us to relax, use the rug, walk on it; it's not sacred. When it gets dirty, we clean it."

"Okay, he might have initiated the rug for the dog world, but no other humans are going to be before us," I said, taking Joy by the hand.

We went upstairs, put on shoes and spent the next five minutes marching back and forth on the new rug. Fitzgo's eyes followed us as we walked back and forth. He got up and gave us his stretch, first the front paws way out, then the back. Over the months Fitzgo's stretch had become the "when in doubt" movement. When he was in doubt about whether he was doing something right, or after he had been scolded, he would stretch.

"It's okay, Fitz," I called to him, and he joined us as we marched back and forth, breaking in the new rug.

The newly refinished house took some getting used to for all of us. Joy and I weren't used to clothes that didn't have plaster dust on them, furniture without drop-cloths and other simple things in life that most people take for granted.

For Fitzgo, it was less of an adjustment. There had been few obstacles in the house while we were working on it, so he had to start walking around things like chairs and tables and lamps. For a dog, this isn't much of a problem. Fitz only miscalculated once.

One of the last pieces of furniture we uncovered was Joy's piano. Even after it was uncovered and dusted off it was a few weeks before Joy found time to play because there were a lot of details to be completed in the house.

Joy got to play the piano for the first time in the new house one night just as I was taking Fitzgo out for his walk.

When Fitz came in from his walk and I took off his collar, he had a habit of immediately checking on Joy. He would race up the stairs looking for her or would bound into the living room and slip and slide across the wooden floor in the dining area in his pursuit. Each night it was as if he was sure she wasn't going to be there when we got back.

That night, I took the collar off and Fitz took off into the living room, making a fast start on the thick red rug in the hallway. He ran into the living room on his usual path, which took him between the piano and the couch. This time a piano bench was there and, running full tilt, he crashed into one of the legs.

Joy was almost knocked off the bench by the jolt.

Fitz let out a painful yelp. He tucked one leg underneath him, limped a few more steps and collapsed on the floor.

"Paul, he didn't know; oh, Paul, that could kill him," Joy said, going toward the dog, which was lying still on the rug, his eyes closed.

"He's stunned, Joy, he's just stunned," I said, trying to believe my own words. "Give him a couple of minutes."

Fitz just lay there, and finally one eye flickered half open. Joy kept on stroking him and talking softly to him.

"You didn't know, Fitz, you didn't know," Joy was saying.

His eye flickered closed. Then it opened again. And then his other. We both were stroking him, and he looked as if we had caught him in the middle of a nap and he couldn't quite wake up.

His eyes opened wide and he struggled to his feet. He favored the one leg, then began to set it down lightly, then with his full weight. He walked slowly toward his water bowl—he usually got a drink after his walk—and looked over his shoulder at us. He gave his body a slight shake. And the next sound we heard was lapping.

Fitzgo seemed to enjoy it when we were able to have people in. With the house in a turmoil all those months, entertaining had been out of the question. Fitz greeted guests at the door, barking and jumping in the air to do his wiggle. Some of our friends were frightened, but we explained that it was his way of saying hello and that he wouldn't bite.

Fitzgo not only didn't bite, he had beautiful manners. He never pushed himself on people who made it plain they didn't care for dogs. Even people who do like dogs don't like dogs jumping all over them. Fitzgo waited until someone called to him; then he would go to the chair, stand and be petted. As the visit and the conversation got longer, he would curl up in the middle of the rug and go to sleep. (And yes, once we had rugs and I would spend an evening at home reading, Fitzgo would do what I thought any decent dog should: he would curl up at my feet.)

We were always happy to tell how Fitzgo had lived in the park and slept under the warmest car in the winter, how the old man had tamed him, how he was there on the fourth floor on the last possible day that we could have found out about the eviction notice. I thought people might find the story boring after telling it many times over, but it seemed everyone was fascinated by it, and some people were so taken by his story that tears came to their eyes somewhere along the route he traveled from Central Park to Brooklyn.

People began to see things in Fitzgo that at times charmed us, at times embarrassed us. I, for one, don't like to hear people give human characteristics to animals. But what could I say when someone would look at Fitzgo and say, "Now there is a dog with an understanding face; you can just tell he knows what you're thinking or how you're feeling."

"There's a dog with character, with class," the chubby, bald-headed man at the newsstand said almost every morning when I picked up the morning paper on my walk with Fitzgo. "I get all kinds in here, and that dog," he would say, jabbing his finger in Fitzgo's direction and telling anybody who would listen, "that dog has the stuff."

Of course there were jokes about Fitzgo's appearance too, especially about his teeth. Fitzgo's two large teeth on the bottom jaw had gone their separate ways— one jutting out, the other turning in. And his top jaw was a jumble of misshapen and crooked teeth. A friend of ours looked at Fitzgo one night and gave the best description: "Either that dog is smiling or his face is caught on his teeth."

Joy and I laughed heartily and looked at Fitzgo. His bottom teeth puckered up his jowl, and it really did look as if he were smiling at us—or, indeed, as if part of his face was caught. Fitzgo stretched in return. He didn't know why we were pointing at him and laughing. And when he straightened up, his jowls and his dignity were back in place.

Chapter Fourteen

O N A WARM Saturday afternoon in the fall we decided
to drive with some friends north of the city where the
leaves were beginning to turn. We planned to stop at a
state park and then to go on to a country inn for dinner.

By two o'clock we were ready. I opened up the back
of our car, and Fitzgo jumped in and immediately started
huffing. By this time we hardly noticed it except when
he would huff so hard that moisture would roll off his
tongue and drop down the backs of our necks or on our
arms.

"Fitz, you'd better relax," I said. "We're going to
be driving for a couple of hours."

"And if your tongue gets out farther and farther as
we go, you're going to be stepping on it before we're
there," Joy added.

As we drove through the city streets, Fitz's eyes

scanned the sidewalks. He could see five dogs before he would bark at one. And we knew, when he did bark, what kind of dog to look for. Purebred dogs—elegant collies, menacing Dobermans, little poodles—never got a rise out of Fitzgo. When he barked we looked for a mongrel, a mutt; there would always be one around. Fitzgo knew his own kind, and it seemed as though they were the ones he wanted to communicate with.

So often they were dogs, like Fitzgo, that gave us no hint as to what breeds were on their family tree. Just plain old dogs, spotted, some of faded colors—usually between a tan and brown—or patched, like Fitzgo. Some of them would be on leashes. Many were dogs of the street, dogs with their ribs showing who slunk along in the shadows of buildings, sometimes limping on three legs, most of the time with their tails between their legs. Fitzgo, in whatever ways dogs sense these things, knew what they were up against and somehow, Joy told me, he wanted to give them some encouragement to go on, to keep fighting, not to give up and let the city beat them.

Once we were out of the city, that special air of autumn filled our car: the smell of pines and brown leaves, a full and hearty smell. Fitzgo sniffed at the air as it came through an opening in the window. It was probably his first ride outside the city, so the air must have contained scents he'd never experienced before.

Toward the end of the afternoon we stopped at the state park that was all but deserted because it officially had closed on Labor Day. There was a chain across the entrance, so we and our friends parked our cars and began to walk down the road toward a lake that we could see in the distance.

Fitzgo loped along beside us for a while, then ran out ahead on the grass beside the road. He had a funny way of running—we had seen him do this before in Prospect Park—where he would race very fast, keeping his face just inches off the ground, obviously following a scent. He looked like a canine vacuum cleaner. We often wondered why he never ran into anything or bumped his nose on a sudden rise in the ground.

Fitz would run out ahead; then, almost as if he had reached the end of a string, he'd come running back to us, only to take off once again.

As we reached the top of a gentle slope that led down to the lake, one of our friends said, "We might be a little early, but deer like to come down to the lake around sunset to drink. I've seen them here many times. You got a deer chaser there?"

"No," I said. "Fitz wouldn't know what to do if he saw one. On the way out we saw some cows and horses and Fitz didn't even bark. He couldn't believe they were real, I don't think. Cats are his favorite. Cats he'll chase for sure. Any mountain lions up here?"

We sat down close to the lake, which was without a ripple on the windless day, and we could see the trees on the other side reflected—bright oranges and reds and yellows. Fitzgo went down to the lake for a drink just as our friends said softly, "There's one."

"Where?" we chimed in.

"Straight across the lake, right in front of us. See it?"

We strained to pick the deer out of the shadows on the other side of the lake. Finally we could make it out: a young fawn just finishing her drink and looking in our direction.

"Fitzgo," I called to him. He came running to us. I pointed his head in the direction of the fawn. "That, my friend, is a deer."

Fitzgo was looking in the deer's direction, but he didn't seem to be interested in it. He went back to the lake for another drink of water.

"Look," another of our friends whispered. We all turned around to see a young buck with a five- or seven-point set of antlers standing on the ridge behind us.

"What a beauty he is!" Joy exclaimed. "I hope he makes it through the hunting season."

The buck just stood there, looking at us, then moved his head as if he were looking in the fawn's direction.

Suddenly I heard the rustle of leaves and the rapid beat of Fitzgo's paws. He streaked right by us, headed for the buck. The deer turned quickly and bounded across a row of hedges and out of sight over the hill. Fitzgo, without sounding a bark, was hot in pursuit.

"Let him have a run. It'll do him good," I said, laughing, to our friends.

Joy was more concerned. "I sure hope he doesn't follow him and get lost in there." Then she smiled too. "No, that deer will lose him in a minute."

We went up over the ridge to see if we could see

either the deer or Fitzgo. But all there was in front of us was a small sloping field of wild grass and, beyond it, a dark, thick forest.

"Fitz!" I called out, at first not too loudly, because I expected him to come running back as he always had done before. We looked across the wild grass and into the woods beyond. Nothing came back except echoes of my weak calls.

After fifteen minutes of walking slowly and joking halfheartedly that the deer would outdistance Fitz in a minute, and every so often calling out to our dog, my wife put into words the thoughts that were then starting to creep into all our minds.

"He . . . you know . . . he could get lost out there. How does he know where we are?"

"Okay, let's keep our heads and give him a chance to find us," I said. "Fran and Jerry, you stay on the road in plain view, so if he comes out he'll see you. George and Karol, you branch off to the left into the woods, and Joy and I will go to the right. If somebody doesn't turn him up, let's meet back here in a half hour. Now there's nothing to worry about; he'll be right back."

"Fitz, Fitzgo," six voices of varying strengths and tones called out. The echoes resounded through the forest. "Come out, Fitz. Good dog. Come on back."

The shadows of the trees lengthened to the road, and the warm afternoon breeze suddenly turned to an autumn chill.

"Fitz! Fitzgo! Here we are, Fitzgo," I called out. But after fifteen minutes my voice and Joy's were getting weak and hoarse.

We met back on the road with our friends and decided that one person should stay on the road in plain view in case Fitzgo came out. We also decided we could cover more ground if the other five fanned out into the woods. We were to meet an hour later.

We went in different directions, not really knowing which way the deer and Fitzgo had gone after they'd left the ridge. Again our weakening voices called out, "Fitz! Fitzgo!"

Less than an hour later we could no longer see well enough in the woods, so we called our friends together. We were afraid one of them might get lost looking for the dog which, Joy and I now silently admitted to ourselves, was lost.

The six of us trudged back along the road toward the cars. Every so often one of us would let go with a hoarse "Fitzgo!" but other than that we said nothing.

When we got back to the cars, we began to lay plans. One couple would go out to get food and bring it back. We would stay in our car, leaving the lights on, hoping Fitzgo might see us.

"But there are lights on the road; how will he ever know that this set of headlights is ours?" Joy said in a thick voice, her eyes beginning to glisten.

"I don't know. I honestly don't know," I said. "We just have to hope for the best."

We planned to stay until midnight at the park.

Then we would find a motel nearby and come back first thing in the morning and—if we had to—spend the next day looking for Fitzgo. Our friends volunteered to stay but we knew both couples needed to get home that night.

"He could be lying out there hurt; even if he heard us he couldn't do anything about it," Joy said. This time she was in tears.

I couldn't think of anything to say. I just looked out at the huge dark state park and the old man suddenly flashed into my mind. "Maybe the wild dog had to return to the wild," I said slowly. "He made it a year in Central Park. Maybe he can live out there. Maybe he'll find a house or a farm nearby and they'll take him in."

"Maybe," I said, clearing my throat, "Fitzgo was never meant to belong to anyone for a long time."

I could see the tears running down Joy's cheeks as we stood in front of the car headlights. "It's getting cold," I said. "Let's get inside and start the heater and wait."

"I almost hate to think of being warm when Fitzgo's out there—" She stopped suddenly.

We both saw it at the same time, but neither of us spoke. We couldn't make out just what it was. But far down the road, at the point where the headlights faded into the darkness, we could see a white dot. It could have been a piece of paper. It could have been a white stone.

We stared. And still we said nothing as the white spot seemed to get larger. And larger. And larger.

It was Fitz.

His tail was between his mud-streaked legs, and he was walking toward us as if he wasn't sure he would be welcomed back.

"Fitz, Fitz!" Joy called out. The dog quickened his pace to a trot. "Oh, my Fitzgo," she said dropping to her knees.

Burrs and small twigs were stuck in his fur. And his tongue! We had never seen it hanging out that far before. His sides were heaving as if he couldn't get enough air.

"We left him so far out there, how could he have ever found us way over . . . Oh, it doesn't matter," Joy said. "He's back. He didn't return to the wild. He wants to stay with us!"

Fitzgo huffed for the first half hour of the two-hour trip back to the city. Then he stopped, lay down and fell asleep. Not even when the tires hit the grating on the Brooklyn Bridge, giving off the high-pitched whine, did Fitz wake up.

Photo by Vaccaro, Staff Editorial